MARKETING DECISIONS AND STRATEGIES
An International Perspective

Adonis & Abbey Publishers Ltd/Skylark Publications (Ghana)
St James House
13 Kensington Square,
London, W8 5HD
United Kingdom

Website: http://www.adonis-abbey.com
E-mail Address: editor@adonis-abbey.com

Nigeria:
Suites C4 & C5 J-Plus Plaza
Asokoro, Abuja, Nigeria
Tel: +234 (0) 7058078841/08052035034

British Library Cataloguing-in-Publication Data
A catalogue record for this book is available from the British Library

ISBN: 978-1-909112-61-2

MARKETING DECISIONS AND STRATEGIES
An International Perspective

John Kuada

Dedication

Affectionately dedicated to

GITTE, ESI AND SENYO

For their patience, understanding and support

PREFACE

Background

A widespread assumption in business and economics is that individuals, households, and organizations always make rational (reasonable and logical) decisions. The process is assumed to start with the identification of needs or problems, development of alternative solutions and the selection of the best among them. From a marketing perspective, executive decisions that seek to improve marketing performance entail understanding environmental and market opportunities and challenges, examining available options, identifying market potentials, and formulating appropriate marketing strategies. This perspective implicitly sees the environments within which companies carry out their functions to be essentially knowable and predictable. This enables managers to make marketing decisions with relative certainty about their outcomes.

In real life, the decision making process is not as straight forward as some scholars present it. It is commonly known that managers make decisions "in-action" – i.e. they grapple with critical problems on daily basis and make decisions to resolve them in order to keep their organizations running. Some of these decisions are made on the basis of elaborate analysis and sometimes on the basis of experience and interactions with other people. The same holds true for consumers as well. Humans have only limited time, information, and cognitive capacity to make some important decisions in life, including purchase decisions. Thus, they must accept some risk of making a less optimal decision.This means satisfactory decision making and sound common sense are completely compatible. In other words, intuition and analysis are the two most powerful techniques for decision making and their connection is often synergistic. Analysis allows individuals to address issues unfamiliar to them in a systematic manner while intuition guides the analysis and helps them to draw on their experiences in making sense of the new information available to them.

Focus of the Book

This book seeks to highlight the view that it is legitimate for managers to combine rational processes with intuition, rules of thumb, and judgments in making decision in even complex situations. It discusses how managers combine the rational and non-rational decision making processes, drawing attention to the tools that help them in the process and the implications that this has for their marketing strategy formulation, especially in international business contexts. Furthermore, it seeks to emphasize the point that marketing management (like other facets of management) is basically a human activity and human beings must be at centre stage of all managerial discussions – right from executive decision making to frontline employees' handling of consumer complaints. Thus, the book also endorses the distinction between internal and external marketing. From an internal marketing perspective, employees must be seen and treated in the same manner as companies treat their customers. They must be provided appropriate skills and resources and be motivated as well as empowered for them to serve customers effectively. In other words, the task of hiring, training, retaining, motivating employees is as just a marketing function as it is a human resource function.

In terms of structure the books starts in chapter one with a discussion of the operational environments in which marketing decisions are made. This is followed by discussions of the concept of marketing strategy in chapter two, and rational approaches to market knowledge acquisition in chapter three. These discussions formed the backdrop for the presentation of a framework for foreign market opportunity analysis in chapter four. Chapter five discusses marketing driving strategies while chapter six provides an overview of the concept of internal marketing and market-oriented strategies. Chapter seven introduces relational approaches to marketing; chapter eight discusses organizational buying behaviour and strategies and chapter nine presents different perspectives on online advertising decisions and strategies. Chapters ten and eleven focus attention on assessment of export market opportunities and entry mode strategies. New developments in the marketing literature draw attention to marketing opportunities and challenges in emerging market economies and social (as well as ethical) concerns in international marketing. These issues are discussed in chapters twelve and thirteen respectively.

ACKNOWLEDGEMENTS

This book would not have been written without the help and generosity of several people. My colleagues at the International Business Centre (Aalborg University) have provided me with an enriching academic atmosphere and have consistently engaged in stimulating intellectual conversations with me. My sincere thanks go to all of them. During the process of the writing itself many of my colleagues and students have provided me with invaluable assistance at each stage. They have saved me from serious errors and compelled me to think through the implications of some of my arguments. Let me add in the same breath, however, that all factual errors and errors of perception and analysis in the dissertation remain solely my responsibility.

Finally, I would like to acknowledge my profound gratitude to my wife and children without whose encouragement and support the book would not have been completed. To them, I extend my sincere thanks.

Table of Contents

CHAPTER ONE

Marketing Decision Making in Dynamic Operational Environment

1.1 Introduction

During the past 50 years, management scholars have developed tools and models for the evaluation of options that executives may have to consider in different situations before making decisions. These tools and models generally assume that well-informed decisions require managers (and/or their assistants) to gather, sift, and analyse information from both internal and external sources and use this set of information to guide their strategic decisions. From a decision making perspective, companies tend to rely on few experts with skills in bringing together and analysing varieties of data and depending on information technology to ensure that information flows more smoothly and quickly within companies. Making meaningful and effective decisions therefore entails engagement with employees and with knowledgeable persons that are within their professional and/or social networks. Not all managers and scholars endorse this structured view of strategic decision making. Practitioners argue that the operational environments of businesses are essentially unknowable, and unpredictable. As such, they cannot be fully quantified and managed with the use of structured models. This means the quality of management decisions will, to a large extent, rest on the problem-solving skills of individual managers. This perspective provides justification for a deeper insight into cognitive processes of decision making as well as decision making styles, behaviours, and personality characteristics that influence decision making. It also requires an understanding of the manner in which individuals make decisions under different environmental conditions.

This chapter seeks to provide you with an overview of some of the leading issues taken up in executive decision making research, particularly with reference to the impact of behavioural and environmental characteristics on the decision making process of business organizations. It will discuss some of the central theoretical arguments on which decision making studies have been based, including issues such as efficiency/effectiveness objectives of organizations, bounded rationality, cognitive biases, and heuristic judgments. The chapter also discusses how these concepts have influenced the tools and guidelines developed over the years to guide decision making processes.

1.2 Efficiency and Effectiveness Dimensions of Managerial Decisions

Organizations often make important strategic and operational decisions based on how different alternatives will increase or decrease the efficiency or effectiveness of their activities. But many managers find the concepts of efficiency and effectiveness rather confusing since they are frequently used interchangeable both in academic and popular management literature. However, a more consistent application of the definitions of the two concepts should help managers to align expectations about the outcomes of their decisions with real performance in terms of profitability and long term sustainability. This section of the chapter provides some clarity in the definition and usage of the concepts and explains their implications for management decisions, in general, and marketing in particular.

The term *efficiency* is used in management to refer to the measurement of relationship between inputs and outputs or how successfully inputs have been transformed into outputs in an organization. In simple language, efficiency refers to doing things in a right manner – i.e. obtaining maximum output with minimum resources. Economists use the term "economic efficiency" to encompass four sub-classifications of efficiency – productive efficiency, technical efficiency, allocative efficiency, and dynamic efficiency. Productive efficiency is achieved when output is produced at minimum cost. That is, a productively efficient outcome uses the least cost input mix required to produce a given output of any good or service. Productive efficiency incorporates technical efficiency, which refers to the extent to which it is technically feasible to reduce any input without decreasing the output, and without increasing any other input in the input mix. Allocative efficiency is about ensuring that an entity (e.g. an organization or a community) gets the greatest return from its scarce resources. Dynamic efficiency refers to the allocation of resources over time, including allocations designed to improve economic efficiency and to generate more resources. Dynamic efficiency may therefore directly impact the long term survival of the company.

There are other classifications of efficiency in the business literature. For example, Pinprayong and Siengthai (2012) draw a distinction between business efficiency and organizational efficiency. To them business efficiency reveals the performance of input and output ratio (i.e. cost performance), while organizational efficiency reflects the improvement of internal processes of an organization, such as organizational structure, culture and management styles. Decisions taken to reduce inventory waste, to increase productivity, or share facilities within an organization will all qualify as decisions aimed at greater business efficiency since they contribute to overall reduction in input usage in the organization. Excellent organizational efficiency such as management styles can enhance employee job satisfaction, motivation, and commitment and could improve an organization's overall performance. Thus, business and organizational efficiencies are closely linked.

The term *effectiveness* relates to the vision and mission of an organization – i.e. the desirables. Effectiveness therefore measures the nature and level of accomplishment within an organization. That is, the extent to which the accomplishments in an organization actually fulfils the goals and expectations of the organization's stakeholders. It builds on what Kuada (2010) refers to as the 3Vs-Vision, Values and Voices. Vision offers purposeful direction – i.e. having a destination. Employees are frequently faced with multiple priorities and without a vision they will end up duplicating their efforts, wasting their energy and therefore becoming inefficient in their operational tasks. As Blanchard (2007:22) argues, "a vision builds trust, collaboration, motivation and mutual responsibility for success". Organizational and leadership values serve as the guideposts in organizations, just as societal values inform members of a society about what they should see as "right" and "wrong". Said differently, values remind employees of the inherent meaning of their jobs and provide them with guidelines on how they should go about their work. Voice gives employees empowerment and allows them to relate closely with the executives, providing essential feedback on changes on the ground. Since realities on the ground change over time it is important for executives to listen not only to the voices within themselves but also to those around them. Thus, effectiveness relates to the managerial capability to sense and know the "right things" to do and to guide the organization as a whole to do those "right things" in the right manner. This also means the term effectiveness helps management to keep the long term sustainability of the organization in mind, be aware of the dynamics of the environment and adapt accordingly to them. In marketing terms, effectiveness means anticipating the needs of customers (sometimes even before customers are aware of these needs themselves) and developing service propositions that fulfil these needs.

Crudely put, an organization may be assessed as having high or low degrees of efficiency and effectiveness. These assessments can be schematically presented in a 2 X 2 matrix as shown in Figure 1.1. The best run organizations are those in which decisions are madeto ensure both high levels of effectiveness and efficiency. Such organizations demonstrate excellence in their operational performance as well as strategic management decisions. They will usually have costs under control, employees will be well aware of the tasks they have been delegated to perform and these will be completed in a timely manner. This means most of the employees will show high levels of commitment and morale, and the long term goals and vision of the organization will be a source of inspiration and energy for their work.

Figure 1.1 Efficiency and Effectiveness Dimensions of Managerial Decisions

		Effectiveness	
		High	**Low**
Efficiency	**High**	Consistently high performing organizations (demonstrate innovativeness and adaptability).	Organizations characterized by roles, authority structures and routines
	Low	Entrepreneurial and ideologically committed organizations	Consistently low performing organizations (Lacking vision, direction , motivation and skills)

If an organization exhibits low levels of efficiency but is highly effective it might survive, but its cost of operational management and inputs will be suboptimal and this will impact its overall performance. A company with such characteristics may be innovative and capture market shares from competitors, but might do so with high operational costs – barely breaking even or having very little profit. Usually, employee morale in such organizations will be high. But its overall survival is questionable.

Organizations that are low in effectiveness but high in efficiency tend to be focused on immediate tasks and their employees tend to exhibit high work discipline and skills that ensure optimal use of resources. Their short run operational (financial) performances will be high. But their employees will be mostly involved in routine tasks - their creative capacity will remain nearly unexplored. Such organizations may experience strategic drift from the environment in the long run. This will put their long run sustainability in jeopardy. Organizations which are low on both efficiency and effectiveness will show consistently low performances. Their employees will exhibit low morale and low capacity to be innovative and/or explore new opportunities.

The discussions above suggest that key management decisions in all organizations must aim at raising both their efficiency and effectiveness levels concurrently. It is, however, important to note that the position of the decision maker in the organizational hierarchy will influence the extent to which he or she will be more concerned with effectiveness or efficiency related decisions. Top executives are normally required to focus attention on ensuring an organization's effectiveness, looking beyond immediate task performance and exploring opportunities for long term growth and sustainability. Managers at lower levels of the organizational hierarchy tend to be more concerned with efficiency related decisions, making sure that the tasks at hand are carried out with minimum possible resources without overstraining employees' capacities and jeopardizing their job satisfaction. Middle level managers perform the key role of balancing effectiveness and efficiency. They are the interpreters of top executive visions and goals and relating them to the capacity and resources available on the ground. The successful performance of the balancing role determines whether an organization can maintain its internal cohesion and exploit existing resources optimally and at the same time consistently alignment organizational activities to the expectations of the external stakeholders.

1.3 Efficiency and Effectiveness Strategies in Marketing

Seen from marketing perspective, the main goal of an organization is to identify market opportunities that raise a company's values and ensure its sustainability in the long run. To do so, companies are expected to find a suitable market niche in order to be productive and competitive in a given external environment. These expectations are often described in the marketing textbooks as finding appropriate "breadwinners" for companies. Doing so requires that marketing managers must develop methodological approaches suitable for continuous assessment and monitoring of all key environmental forces since these forces change dynamically as companies expand their operations at home and abroad. That is, the content and the intensity of external operational conditions vary from one country or region to another depending on how stakeholders in each country represent their interests and shape the social and political environments.

Efficiency in marketing strategy formulation relates to paying attention to marketing resources. A basic rule is that a company should avoid covering too many markets and over extending itself, since this will leave the company vulnerable to competitor attacks. A company that is trying to cover all bases may face one or more of the following difficulties. First, a company, especially a small one, may not have the resources to offer a full product line. Second, product proliferation may cause a company to spread its resources too thinly, violating the principle of concentration of forces at the decisive point. Third, this strategy makes the company an easy target for attack by competitors. Even if a company was able to cover the major segments, it is impossible to cover every possible niche in the market.

1.3.1 The BCG Model

The Boston Consultancy Group's (BCG) product classification in terms of "stars", "question marks", cash-cows" and "dogs", provides a simple but useful overview of how companies must strive for efficiency as well as effectiveness in their product/service portfolio. This classification is presented below for a quick overview.

"Stars" consititute a company's new/innovative products and services that provide values that its customers did not anticipate. They reflect the company's capacity to make decisions that explore opportunities that are barely incipient and therefore provide it with a first mover advantage. As long as the company can hold competitors off, it can establish itself effectively in that business area. It is, however, important to realise that such propositions are risky. The company is likely to be a pioneer in the specific line of business and its potential customers many have no knowledge of how valuable the goods and services are. Many of them will, therefore, show substantial uncertainties about deciding to try them. This requires the company to emphasise persuasion in its marketing strategy – i.e. encouraging the customers to give the new goods and services a try.

"Cash cows" are products and services that customers are familiar with and demand. This is an area where efficiency is highly important. Costs must be reduced, quality must be guaranteed, delivery systems and prices must be aligned to customer expectations and customer complaints (if they occur) must be handled swiftly and satisfactorily. The strategic goal is to ensure high market shares and profits based on superior ability to serve customers.

"Question mark" products and services are also known as *problem children*. They are classified as such because they have shown disappointing performances on the market. This is an example where the company shows high effectiveness but low efficiency – effectiveness through innovation and new product development, but low efficiency due to limited ability to produce and market the products and services efficiently. Such companies need to find out the reasons for the poor performance and take appropriate actions to strengthen the market acceptability of the goods and services.

"Dogs" are goods and services that are no longer in high demand and require the company to spend more to serve its customers than the customers are willing to pay. It is always advisable to phase out such products quickly or re-launch them as new ones to new target customers who will see them as a "star" of a kind. Decisions must be made that help re-innovate the product in order to sustain its competitive position in the market for a long period of time.

1.3.2 Monitoring Efficiency and Effectiveness with Balanced Scorecard

The balanced scorecard has emerged as a useful decision tool that marketers can use in guiding their efficiency and effectiveness strategies. It requires decision makers to pay attention to the following three issues:

- Set clear objectives with regard to both efficiency and effectiveness

- Collect data to monitor progress and conduct regular analysis
- Take timely corrective actions

Paying attention to these issues enables managers to monitor both current performance and the factors that drive future performance. Marketing performance monitoring focuses on financial, customer, and internal process considerations that influence growth. The financial perspective focuses attention on *return on marketing investment* - i.e. revenue growth and the operational efficiency of the marketing function. With this assessment managers will monitor the extent to which specific customer groups, products, or geographic market areas contribute to revenue. Customer performance monitoring focus on goals related to customer acquisition and to customer retention, growth, and satisfaction. It helps managers monitor the *number of new customers acquired* (or number of new customers of a particular type). The internal measures relate to the dissemination of information collected about current and potential customers within the organization and how the information influences strategy formulation and implementation. In this way it helps streamline the communication mix that companies use to inform prospects and customers about the company's value propositions. These measures also help a company to gain insights into the types of employee capabilities, information systems, and organizational capabilities it needs to continually improve its processes and sustain growth.

1.4   Decision Making Environments

The efficiency/effectiveness discussions above suggest that decision makers must always be mindful of organizational visions, goals and resources in all the decisions they make. It also implies that stakeholders' expectations and changes within the operational environment must be consistently monitored for the decisions to impact performance positively. Mangers are therefore continuously reminded that all organizations operate in well-defined external environments set by national boundaries or lawfully established geographic regions. It is therefore important for them to understand how individual environmental forces impact their strategic and operational decisions.

Seen from management decision making perspective the environmental forces may be classified into three groups: certain, risky, and uncertain. As we shall argue below, the term uncertainty is used in the literature to describe possible outcomes that are unknown, while risk refers to a certain type of uncertainty that involves the real possibility of loss. Risks can be more comprehensively accounted for than uncertainty. It is generally acknowledged that decision makers' preferences change under these three different situations. For example, certainty may allow for rational decisions. But as the level of certainty changes, it is common to find that conclusions that are reached by rational deliberations may be overridden by strong emotional impulses, thereby altering original preferences. The three environmental conditions are briefly explained below.

1.4.1 Certainty

Decisions are said to be made under the condition of certainty when the manager has perfect knowledge of all the information needed to make a decision. The decision maker's main task under this condition is simply to study the alternatives and choose the best solution. He or she will be fully sure that the outcome will be what is expected. It is, however, very difficult to find complete certainty in most of the business decisions, except in the most routine-like situations. A good example is the decision to reorder inventory automatically when stock falls below a determined level. Inventory management problems of this type tend to arise on a regular basis, and there is a number of computer-aided decision support software that helps managers to address such problems. Managers may also depend on past experiences to guide them in their choice of appropriate solutions.

1.4.2 Risk

Risk is a fairly common decision condition for managers. It refers to likelihood and impact of an event with the potential to influence organizational performance (Luce and Raiffa, 1957). This definition implies that it is important to incorporate both the probability of the event occurring and the consequences of the event in a definition of risk. That is, some form of quantitative or qualitative analysis is required for assessing the magnitude and impact of risk on the achievement of an organization's objectives. Thus, risk analysis usually assumes that decision makers have adequate information to assign probability to the happening or not happening of each possible event. It is important to note that the probability of some events occurring may be relatively small but the consequences can be catastrophic and this will justify its classification as a high-risk event. A good example is earthquake.

The literature draws distinction between objective and subjective interpretations of probability. The objective interpretation holds that probabilities are real and may be estimated through statistical analyses. The subjective perspective holds that probabilities are human beliefs that may be based on an individual's personal judgement about the likelihood of an event occurring. Such a judgement may be based on past experiences. A manager can therefore anticipate some risky events in the future and make plans to mitigate their impact on organizational goal attainment.

Since risks are inevitable in organizational life, the decision maker does not aim at eliminating them altogether but to understand and manage them as effectively as time and resources permit. Thus, one of the key strategic decisions that executives are required to make is to determine how much risk to take and what type of risks to take. It is often said that managers that decide to protect their organizations against all risk are unlikely to take advantage of emerging opportunities but, organizations that expose themselves to high risk events may fail to attain their objectives. Risk management is therefore a balancing act that requires continuous, proactive and systematic process of analysing, interpreting and taking action timeously to reduce impacts.

Most marketing problems are characterized by cases of partial ignorance in which the decision maker deals with what may be considered a unique situation. This creates risk. Following Green and Tull (1966:27) "the level of risk is higher in marketing than in other functional areas of management both because of the relative scarcity of information and the amount of money spent as a result of marketing decisions". In companies where all other management decisions are based on marketing decisions, marketing costs tend to be quite high–

often estimated to account for more than half of the final costs of goods and services. Prudent marketing decisions do bring in substantial revenues and greatly influence the long-run sustainability of companies. But as noted earlier, marketing cost must be continuously monitored to ensure high degree of operational efficiency in companies. It is often argued that the amount of information required by executives in a decision making process depends on the degree of uncertainty they perceive – the greater the uncertainty as to which possible event will occur, the greater the amount of information they require.

1.4.3 Uncertainty

While risk may be described as conditions of partial uncertainty, managers are sometimes compelled to make decision under complete uncertainty. Lorenzi (1980) describes uncertainty as a set of events that the decision maker believes can occur but has no realistic means of making any prediction about its occurrence. Since he or she cannot assign probabilities to the occurrence of the events, the decision maker cannot predict the outcome of decisions that may be taken (Luce and Raiffa, 1957). Such situations generally arise in cases where the occurrence of the event is determined by external factors – i.e. the company has absolutely no control over its occurrence. For example, possible actions of competitors can hardly be predicted. Uncertainty forces managers to rely heavily on creativity in solving such problems – i.e. thinking outside the boxes, so to speak.

There are multiple sources of uncertainty in business environments. For instance, the introduction of new technologies may change the way businesses operate. This happened with the emergence of the Internet in the late 1980s. Furthermore, a government policy which regulates or deregulates an industry also serves to introduce uncertainties and alter rules of the game within the industry. These changes affect the nature of competition by increasing the array of activities, as well as the heterogeneity of actors within industries.

1.5 Cognitive and Behavioural Dispositions of Decision Makers

The three conditions outlined above tend to challenge decision makers' appetite for risk and this may prove rewarding or otherwise for the organizations in which they work. The differences in decision makers' risk orientations may be ascribed to their cognitive structures and biases. For example, it has been argued that people select, evaluate and use incoming information according to their cognitive maps or structures. Following Nyström, (1974) a cognitive structure may be defined as a set of partially ordered cognitive elements or ideas which are viewed by the decision-maker as relevant for determining the outcome of a contemplated decision. The relations between the elements may be either implicit or viewed as being in an explicit cause and effect relationship to each other. Cognitive structures have inherent biases. Major examples of such biases include memory confirmation and judgment biases. Confirmation bias is said to occur when the decision maker favours information that confirms previously existing beliefs or biases. Confirmation biases impact how people gather information, but they also influence how people interpret and recall information. Judgement biases are the results of human learned behaviour that allow us to use shortcuts in arriving at complex decisions – heuristics or judgments. These shortcuts may result in systematic errors. For example, it may make a decision maker overconfident about the occurrence of an outcome and thereby take a highly risky decicion. These examples of biases reflect the fundamental problem of cognitive limitations of human minds, as well as the time constraints within which key decisions are normally taken (Woiceshyn, 2009).

1.5.1 Uncertainty Gaps and Bounded Rationality

Nyström (1974) suggests that decision makers may experience "uncertainty gaps" between their cognitive structures and their beliefs that these structures provide accurate representation of the realities of their decision environments. A decision maker who experiences such a gap is certain that he cannot make a rational decision and is therefore likely to seek more information. If the decision-maker believes that his cognitive structure is an accurate and sufficient representation of relevant factors (i.e. he experiences no uncertainty gap) he will not seek new information.

Those who hold the view that decision makers must make consistently rational decisions implicitly assume that these decision makers have unlimited cognitive capabilities. This is an unrealistic assumption. The biases discussed above imply that human beings are bound by their cognitive limitations to make sub-optimal decisions. Simon's (1957) concept of bounded rationality seeks to draw attention to this human constraint. He argues that the limitation of the availability of information, the general limitations of cognitive capacities to sift through available information, the intractability of decision problems, and the time required for decisions to be made, all contribute to making individuals "bounded rational" in their decision making. Under such conditions the decisions makers tend to become "satisficers" (i.e. seek satisfactory solutions rather than an optimal one). In other words, sub-optimal decisions are not irrational simply because they fail to conform to norms of full rationality.

Building on this perspective it has been argued that decision makers may exhibit different aspiration levels in different decision situations. That is to say, aspiration levels are not fixed once and for all, but dynamically adjusted to the situation; they are raised, if it is easy to find satisfactory alternatives and lowered if satisfactory alternatives are hard to come by. Decision makers may also vary in terms of the degree of information incompleteness they are likely to tolerate for certain types of problems. If the information incompleteness they experience exceeds the threshold they have set for themselves, they are likely to postpone decision making.

1.5.2 Intuition, Experience and Rational Analysis

Cognitive psychologists inform that decision makers combine intuition and rational analysis when making decisions in risky environments. As noted earlier, Simon (1957) suggested that most human decision making processes are characterized by individuals (or groups) processing only limited, manageable amounts of information rather than identifying all alternatives. They also very often use shortcuts and rules of thumb when processing information. Intuition helps decision makers to identify familiar cues in new situations by drawing on their memories for similarities that the current situation may have with previous ones. This facilitates decision making in even complex situations. The process of using intuition in decision making has been labelled "intuiting", and this involves subconscious reflections. The understanding is that when the conscious mind acquires vast amounts of knowledge that it is impossible to hold in focal awareness simultaneously, much of this information is stored in the subconscious memory. Intuitive processing entails retrieving the information on recall (Woiceshyn, 2009). It has also been shown that experience is a highly useful tool for making good decisions. Experience here refers to the aggregate of what individuals have learned from the process of dealing with problems and making decisions in the course of their lives (Pretz, 2008). Experiences may be memories of actual events and may be transformed into rules of thumb, and judgments. Over time they become integral parts of intuition, instinct or "common sense".

The combination of intuition and rationality may evolve as procedure-based decision making, where decision makers develop a procedure for comparing the problems they face to similar problems that they have solved in the past. Woiceshyn's (2009) study showed that experienced and successful executives use a combination of intuition and rational analysis while making decisions. She labels the process "spiraling". Spiraling is an iterative process of interplay between rational analysis and intuitive reflections that result in a management decision. It works this way: In the first loop of the spiral, decision makers immediately engage with and focus on the decision scenario. Instead of methodical analysis, they took a quick overview of the scenario, grasping it as a whole. They then focus quickly on what they considered the most feasible option(s) and reject the non-feasible ones. In her view, decision makers are able to do so because their intuition brings up rationally classified, essential knowledge from their subconscious memory. In the second loop of the spiral, effective decision makers analyse alternatives by applying principles to reach potential decisions. Examples of these principles include efficiency requirement (e.g. cost), customer satisfaction, and fairness. Finally, in the third loop of the spiral, the decision makers test their tentative decision: they develop additional alternatives, or combinations of alternatives, drawing from their previously integrated knowledge. Once the decision makers identify the essence of their companies' problems and the principles for solving them, they are able to develop a hierarchy of alternatives that address both short-term and long-term performance of the companies. After organising the alternatives into a hierarchy, a sound decision can then be made. Figure 1.2 provides a schematic illustration of Woiceshyn's spiralling model.

Figure 1.2 Spiralling model of Decision Making

Start
Initiate the process of analysis and reflections

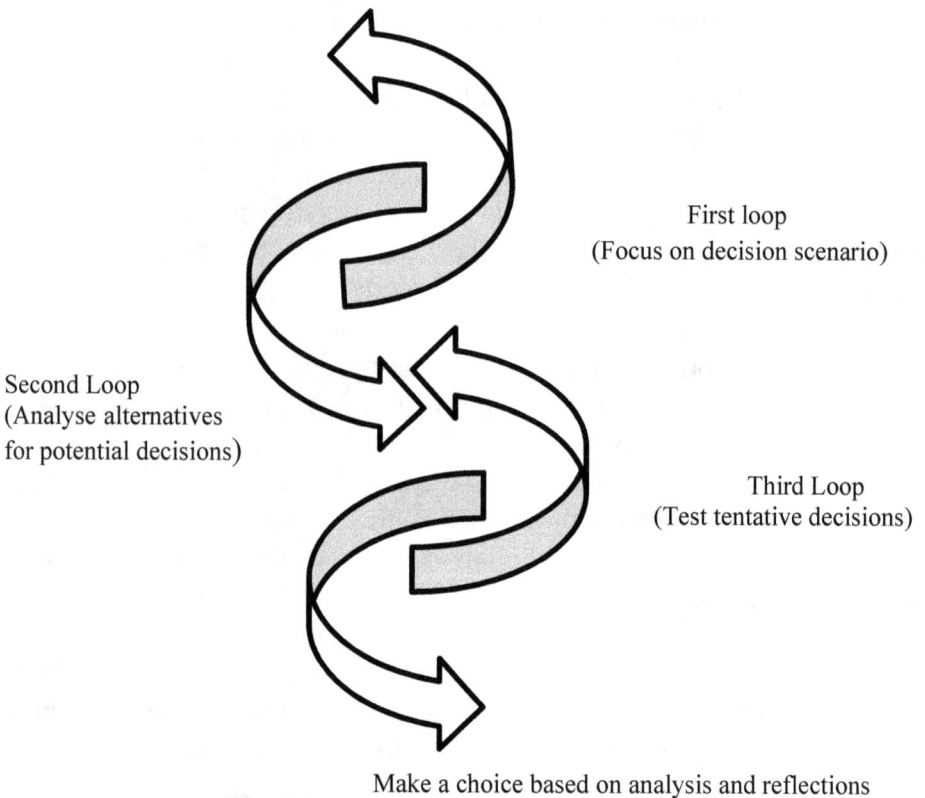

First loop
(Focus on decision scenario)

Second Loop
(Analyse alternatives
for potential decisions)

Third Loop
(Test tentative decisions)

Make a choice based on analysis and reflections

Source: Based on Woiceshyn (2009)

1.5.3   Limitations of Intuition

Some authors caution that reliance on intuition does not always result in high-quality decisions. The argument is that there are many potential sources of cognitive biases that obstruct the decision making process. For example, experience, and the judgment stemming from experience, can be a source of self-esteem and authority. For this reason experienced decision makers may become overconfident and unwittingly apply the lessons of the past to new and dissimilar situations. Box 1.1 provides examples of common cognitive biases that have been noted in decision making processes. However, some particular conditions (e.g. when problems are not well structured, or the organizational environment is unstable) may augur better for intuiting rather than rational analysis. It has also been suggested that some of the weaknesses inherent in intuiting may be compensated for by encouraging executives to resort to the use of "qualified consensus" – i.e. engaging other executives in a discussion process to find a common solution to the problem on hand (see Bourgeois, 1980).

Box 1.1

Examples of Common Cognitive Biases

1. Conjunction fallacy: The tendency to assume that specific conditions are more probable than a single general one
2. Endowment effect: The tendency that people often demand more to give up on an object than they would be willing to pay to acquire it
3. Fundamental attribution error: The tendency to overemphasize personal factors and underestimate situational factors when explaining other people's behaviour
4. Gambler's fallacy: The tendency to think that future probabilities are changed by past events, when in reality they are unchanged (e.g., series of roulette wheel spins)
5. Halo effect: The tendency for a person's positive or negative traits to extend from one area of their personality to another in others' perceptions of them
6. Hindsight bias: A memory distortion phenomenon by which, with the benefit of feedback about the outcome of an event, people's recalled judgments of the likelihood of that event are typically closer to the actual outcome than their original judgments were.
7. Illusory correlation: The tendency to identify a correlation between a certain type of action and effect when no such correlation exists
8. In-group bias: The tendency for people to give preferential treatment to others they perceive to be members of their own group
9. Mere exposure effect: The tendency by which people develop a preference for things merely because they are familiar with them

Based on Wilke A. and Mata R. (2012) "Cognitive Bias" In V.S. Ramachandran (Ed.) *The Encyclopedia of Human Behaviour*, Vol. 1, pp. 531-535. Academic Press

1.6 Executive Personality and Decision Making

Following Brousseau et al. (2006) decision styles differ in two other fundamental ways: how information is used and how options are created. There are executives who would want to have full knowledge of the situations in which they are to operate before making decisions – i.e. they will want to make well informed decisions. The management literature labels such executives "maximizers." The well-informed decision always comes at a cost in terms of time and efficiency – e.g. businesses may lose good opportunities to competitors by delaying their decisions. Other managers just want the key facts as a basis for their decisions. They are willing to make adjustments as additional information becomes available. Herbert Simon will call the latter decision making style as those of "satisficers". With regard to options considered, the available evidence suggests that some managers take one course of action at a time - i.e. they are "single focused" decision makers. Other managers are willing to pursue multiple courses of action at each given point in time – i.e. they are "multifocused". The multi-focused managers are generally adaptive, adjusting their strategies to fit changing circumstances, while their single focused counterparts make determined effort to ensure that things come out as they believe they should.

Managers' propensity to make "well-informed" decisions and/or to adopt single or multi-focused strategies depends partly on their personality and psychological capabilities (Robbins *et al.*, 2009).There are a number of personality classificatory frameworks in the management literature to guide scholars in identifying how executives with specific personality profiles are likely to respond to changes in their operational environments and make decisions. The two dominant ones are the Myers–Briggs Type Indicator and the five-factor model of personality (usually referred to as Big Five model). The Myers–Briggs Type Indicator (MBTI) is based on a 100- question personality test that asks people how they usually feel or act in particular situations. On the basis of the answers individuals give to the test questions, they are classified as extroverted or introverted (E or I), sensing or intuitive (S or N), thinking or feeling (T or F), and judging or perceiving (J or P). These terms are defined as follows:

- *Extroverted versus Introverted*: Extroverted individuals exhibit characteristics such as sociability and assertiveness. Introverts are generally quiet and shy.
- *Sensing versus Intuitive*: Individuals with sensing profiles are practical, they focus on details, and prefer routine and order. Intuitive individuals rely on unconscious processes and look at the big picture.
- *Thinking versus Feeling*: Individuals with "thinking" profiles tend to use reason and logic to handle problems. Feeling types tend to rely on their personal values and emotions.
- *Judging Versus Perceiving*: Individual with dominant "judging" attributes prefer their world to be ordered and structured. Perceiving types are flexible and spontaneous.

The five-factor model of personality identifies the following traits as the most dominant ones:

- *Extroversion* represents sociability and expressiveness. Individuals high in extroversion are generally considered to be outgoing and tend to stimulate social interactions (House and Howell, 1992). They are therefore better at building networks of social relations and leveraging substantial resources through these social ties. Introverts tend to be reserved, timid, and quiet.
- *Conscientiousness* is a personality that reflects thoroughness, a high sense of responsibility and dependability. People who are conscientious are found to be hardworking, achievement-oriented, and their behaviours are goal-directed. They are also dependable and persistent. Those who score low on this dimension are easily distracted, disorganized, and unreliable.
- *Open-mindedness* is associated with traits such as originality, being thoughtful, insightful, imaginative, and flexible. Open-minded managers and employees are likely to be creative, curious, and artistically sensitive. Those at the other end of the openness spectrum are conventional and find comfort in the familiar.
- *Agreeableness* describes a cluster of personality traits that include empathy, courtesy, cooperative, capability, and conflict avoidance. Highly agreeable people are cooperative, warm, and trusting. People who score low on agreeableness are cold, disagreeable, and antagonistic.

- *Neuroticism* refers to the tendency of an individual to experience unpleasant emotions including anxiety, depression, anger, embarrassment, worry, and insecurity. People with positive emotional stability tend to be calm, self-confident, and secure. Those with high negative scores tend to be nervous, anxious, depressed, and insecure.

Building on these classifications, it has been argued that personality differences determine the extent to which individuals define their own rules of behaviour and are able to sense and seize new opportunities in life by attentively exploring their environment. They also explain the extent to which people are able to identify their knowledge gaps and take steps to renew, replace or upgrade their existing knowledge base. For example, managers with high scores on agreeableness, open-mindedness, conscientiousness and extroversion exhibit the desire to lead, but are, at the same time, sensitive to others' emotions. They also tend to be thoughtful, insightful, imaginative, and flexible. These enable them to build coalition among their peers. In this way they pull both tangible and intangible resources within their organizations together in support of their decision. But if successful, they are likely to exhibit tendencies of over-confidence, gradually eroding their support and social capital within their organizations. Extroverts are also noted to interact frequently with a wide variety of people (peers, subordinates and superiors) and take advantage of their cognitive feedback mechanisms to expand and refine their mental schemas through their interactive experiences. Furthermore, when people interact with each other, they cultivate a sense of understanding that helps them collaborate in making decisions and compensate for their individual cognitive biases.

1.6   Summary

An increasing number of scholars and practitioners now hold the view that good decision making encompasses elements of both rational and non-rational perspectives. The understanding is that cognitive baises create errors of perception and interpretation that can result in wrong decisions. This is because, as human beings, we tend to distort our recollections of experiences and their lessons and thereby overestimate the importance of the factors we remember most clearly. Thus, the conclusions we draw on the basis of these experiences may be faulty. For this reason decision makers must avoid relying entirely on automatic cognitive processing mechanisms in new situations. Rational decision making approach has also weaknesses – the operational environment may be too unpredictable to make any rational analysis reliable and efficient. Thus, by applying a careful combination of experience-based and analysis-based decision making procedures managers are more able to solve complex problems, by compensating for the strengths and weaknesses of each.

References

Blanchard, Ken (2007) *Leading at a Higher Level* (New Jersey, FT Press)

Bourgeois, L. J., (1980) "Performance and Consensus" *Strategic Management Journal* Vol.1 No. 1 pp: 227-248

Brousseau, Kenneth R., Driver, Michael J., Hourihan, Gary and Larsson, Rikard (2006) "The Seasoned Executive's Decision-Making Style" *Harvard Business Review* February pp 1-10

Green, Paul E., and Tull, Donald S., (1966) *Research for Marketing Decisions* (New Jersey, Prentice-Hall, Inc)

House, R. J., & Howell, J. M. (1992) "Personality and charismatic leadership" *Leadership Quarterly*, 3, 81-108

Kuada, J. (2010). "Creativity and leadership in a cross-cultural context: the role of expatriates" In J. Kuada, & O. J. Sørensen (Eds), *Culture and creativity in organizations and societies* (pp: 9-23). (London, Adonis & Abbey Publishers Ltd.)

Lorenzi, P., 1980, "Applied Behaviour under Uncertainty" in Seymour Fiddle (Ed) *Uncertainty: behaviour al and Social Dimensions* (New York, Praeger) pp: 284-304

Luce, R. D., and Raiffa, H. (1957) *Games and Decisions: Introduction and Critical Survey* (New York, John Wiley and Sons)

Nyström, Harry (1974) "Uncertainty, Information and Organizational Decision-Making: A Cognitive Approach" *The Swedish Journal of Economics*, Vol. 76, No. 1, pp. 131-139

Pinprayong B. and Siengtai S. (2012) "Restructuring for organizational efficiency in the banking sector in Thailand: A case study of Siam commercial bank"*Far East Journal of Psychology and Business*. Vol. 8 No. 2pp 29-2. http://www.fareastjournals.com/files/FEJPBV 8N2P2.pdf Retrieved 25 January, 2016

Pretz, J.E. (2008) "Intuition versus analysis: Strategy and experience in complex everyday problem solving". *Memory and Cognition*, 36(3): 554-566

Simon, Herbert (1957). "A behaviour al Model of Rational Choice", in Models of Man, Social and Rational: Mathematical Essays on Rational Human behaviour in a Social Setting. New York: Wiley.

Robbins, S.P., Judge, T.A., Odendaal, A., & Roodt, G. (2009) *Organisational Behaviour: Global and Southern African Perspectives* (Cape Town: Pearson Education)

Wilke A., and Mata R. (2012) "Cognitive Bias" In: V.S. Ramachandran (ed.) *TheEncyclopedia of Human behaviour* , Vol. 1, pp. 531-535. (London; Burlington Academic Press).

Woiceshyn, Jaana (2009), "Lessons from "Good Minds": How CEOs Use Intuition, Analysis and Guiding Principles to Make Strategic Decisions," *Long Range Planning*, 42 (3), 298-319.

For Further Readings

Friga, Paul N. and Chapas, Richard B. (2008) "Make Better Business Decisions," *Research – Technology Management* (July-August 2008), 8-16.

Holton, Glyn A., (2004) "Defining Risk" Financial Analysts Journal Vol. 60 No. 6 pp: 19-25

Hopkins, Michael S., (2011) "Why Companies Have to Trade 'Perfect Data' for 'Fast Info'," MIT *Sloan Management Review*, 52/3 pp: 50-6.

Weick, K. E. (1995) *Sensemaking in Organizations* (Thousand Oaks, CA: Sage, 1995)

CHAPTER TWO

The Concept of Strategy in Marketing

2.1 Introduction

Top management's strategic orientation is a primary requirement for successful organizational performance. This orientation is often described in the management literature as a frame of mind that allows management to continuously evaluate and control activities within the organisation and provide it with an overall direction. In business organizations, this strategic orientation must also encourage the management and key employees to regularly assess customer needs and satisfaction with exiting actions as well as assess possible actions that competitors are likely to take. Thus, top management strategic orientation can be described as a foundation for the strategies that companies adopt. Many management scholars see strategy in terms of well-defined sense of mission, foresight and decisions and choices that management makes to guide employees take actions that achieve the objectives of any organization. But there are differences among scholars about how managers strategize – i.e. formulate and implement strategies. These differences are reflected in the marketing literature as well. This chapter gives you an overview of the different perspectives on the concept of strategy and how marketing managers are expected to apply them in their decision making processes.

2.2 The Concept of Strategy

The origin of the concept of strategy can be traced to the Greek word 'strategos', for a general who organises, leads and directs his forces to the most advantageous position (de Wit and Meyer, 2004). In marketing management the term "strategy" is used to describe methods to achieve goals and objectives. As such, it can be considered as the link between actions and events involving top executives and employees with the view to attaining organizational objectives. Stated differently, strategic marketing management answers the following three questions: (1) where do you want your business to go – i.e. goals;

(2) how is your business going to get there – i.e. strategic actions; and (3) how will you know when you get there – i.e. evaluation. The main emphasis of strategy is thus to enable an organisation to achieve competitive advantage with its unique capabilities by focusing on present and future direction of the organisation (Miller, 1991; Kay, 1993). Historically, views of strategy fall into two camps. The first view equates strategy with planning, while the second equates it with thinking and adaptation.

2.2.1 Strategic Planning Perspective

Scholars subscribing to the planning perspective describe strategies as being composed of two essential characteristics: (1) they are made in advance of the actions to which they apply, and (2) they are developed consciously and purposefully. That is, the process is supposed to start with the formulation of what leaders of the organization "plan" to do, and then followed by the actions they are to take to achieve these goals. This conventional understanding implicitly assumes a separation between those with the talent and skills to formulate strategies and those who implement them. Top executives are expected to play a key role in the planning process because they have the skills and broader overview of their organization's vision and direction. The implementation falls into the laps of middle and lower level managers who have the skills and knowledge of specific (tangible and intangible) resources in different parts of their organizations to take the required actions and make adjustments, where necessary.

The benefits of strategic planning include the adoption of systematic approach to decision making and performance measurement, provision of orderly growth and competitive survival, stimulation of organizations to be more responsive to the needs of key stakeholders, increased efficiency, mitigation of crisis-driven decision making, and the improvement of employee morale. The contribution of strategic planning to employee morale must be seen in the light of the clarity of focus, direction, communication, and inclusion that plans offer them.

A strategic planning process consists of a series of steps. These are the most typical among them:

36

1. Establishing a mission statement and key objectives for the organisation.
2. Analysing the external environment (to identify possible opportunities and threats).
3. Conducting an internal organisational analysis (to examine its strengths and weaknesses and the nature of current management systems, competencies and capabilities).
4. Setting specific goals.
5. Examining possible strategic choices / alternatives to achieve organisational objectives and goals.
6. Adoption / implementation of chosen choices.
7. Regular evaluation of actions in terms of efficiency and effectiveness.

These steps emphasize clarity of planning, which entails a division of labour among different levels of management in the initiation, formulation, revision and implementation of plans. Organizations decide whether to include only top management team in the planning process or to encourage diversity in the planning process. Where diversity characterizes the planning process multiple view points are taken into account in the identification of strategic issues and developing solutions.

2.2.2 Strategic Management Perspective

The second perspective is strategic management. This involves looking into the future rather than dwelling on the past. It is usually described as being proactive rather than reactive and emphasizes speed of reaction and flexibility. Proactive dispositions enable organizations to function best in environments that are fast-changing and essentially unpredictable. Thus, the essence of strategy, according to this view, is adaptability and incrementalism.

Some of the key proponents of this perspective include Minztberg and Walters (1982, 1985) who see strategy as a pattern in a stream of decisions. To them, strategies need not be deliberately planned but can emerge as patterns or consistencies in streams of decisions and behaviours which managers and other key employees take. Following this line of thinking, the strategic process can be broken into the following four distinct phases: (1) intended strategy, (2) deliberate strategy, (3) emergent strategy, and (4) realized strategy. *Intended strategies,* are plans conceived by the top management team. This is

37

the component of strategy described by proponents of strategy planning. ***Realized strategies*** constitute those parts of the intended strategies that organizational members are able to implement. The understanding presented by Mintzberg and Walters is that some parts of the intended strategies may not be implemented, possibly because assumptions made in the intended strategy have been found not to hold in reality. ***Emergent strategies*** represent all the strategic decisions that emerge from the complex processes in which individual managers adapt to changing external circumstances and make modifications in the intended strategies. Thus, the realized strategy is a consequence of ***deliberate*** and emerging factors that influence companies' behaviour.

From a business perspective, emergent strategies tend to encourage continuous improvements in costs, product quality, new product development, manufacturing processes, and distribution to fulfil customers' expectations. Marketing managers adopting emergent approaches to strategy formulation are more likely to excite their key customers by taking advantage of situations as and when they occur to go beyond the immediate expectations of these customers without undue extra costs. But this requires empowering sales persons to take initiatives in specific situations. Thus, the flexibility that emergent approach to strategy allows enables management to continuously focus on efficiency dimensions of businesses. For example, low cost company will continuously try to find ways of decreasing costs through economies of scale, cutting costs and introducing new production methods. Companies that pursue differentiation strategies will continuously look for ways to maintain their competitive advantage through innovation, and quality improvements.

Most effective strategies tend to combine planning and control (deliberate strategies) with adaptation, flexibility and incremental learning. In other words, an organization's actual strategy (its realized strategy) is most often the outcome of the adaptation of a plan to emergent issues in the environment. This means the realized strategy can be very different from the strategy as planned.

2.3 The Strategic Process Model

Figure 2.1 provides model of the range of issues that go into the strategy formulation process. The first step in the strategy formulation process is to gain an insight into the organization's current strategic profile as well as administrative heritage. This requires analysis of both internal and external factors that are likely to shape the strategic profile. The analytical process entails answering questions such as: How did the organization reach its present state? Why is it producing its particular range of products and services?

Having gained an understanding of the current situation the analysis will proceed to understand the strategic profile that the organization wants to have within a clearly defined time frame – e.g. three to five years. If it is a business organization, one is likely to ask managers to specify what kind of products or services the company intends to produce in the future – the same or different, and, if different, how different? If it is thinking of altering its current product range, what are the reasons?

Following Dobson *et al* (2004) the analysis also requires executives to answer the following three questions:

1. Are the objectives of the business appropriate?
2. Are the major policies and plans appropriate?
3. Do the results obtained to date conform with or refute critical assumptions on which the strategy rests?

They further suggest that strategy must satisfy four broad criteria:

1. **Consistency**: The strategy must not present mutually inconsistent goals and policies.
2. **Consonance**: The strategy must represent an adaptive response to the external environment and to the critical changes occurring within it.
3. **Advantage**: Strategy must provide for the creation and/or maintenance of a competitive advantage in the selected area of activity.
4. **Feasibility**: The strategy must neither over tax available resources nor create insoluble problems.

Based on the analysis, management lays out the strategic options and assesses the feasibility of each option against its contribution to the attainment of the strategic objectives. This analysis ends up with a choice of specific strategy which then becomes the company's deliberate strategy. Implementation plans are then worked out with the involvement of key employees that will be assigned to the various actions to be taken. Mechanisms will also be put in place to monitor changes within both internal and external environments and the implications that the changes carry for the implementation of the deliberate plans. The changes may necessitate modifications of the original plan in more or less significant forms and shapes. These modifications then define the emergent strategy. The final outcome (i.e. at the end of the implementation time frame) will determine the nature of the realized strategy.

Figure 2.1 The Strategic Process Model

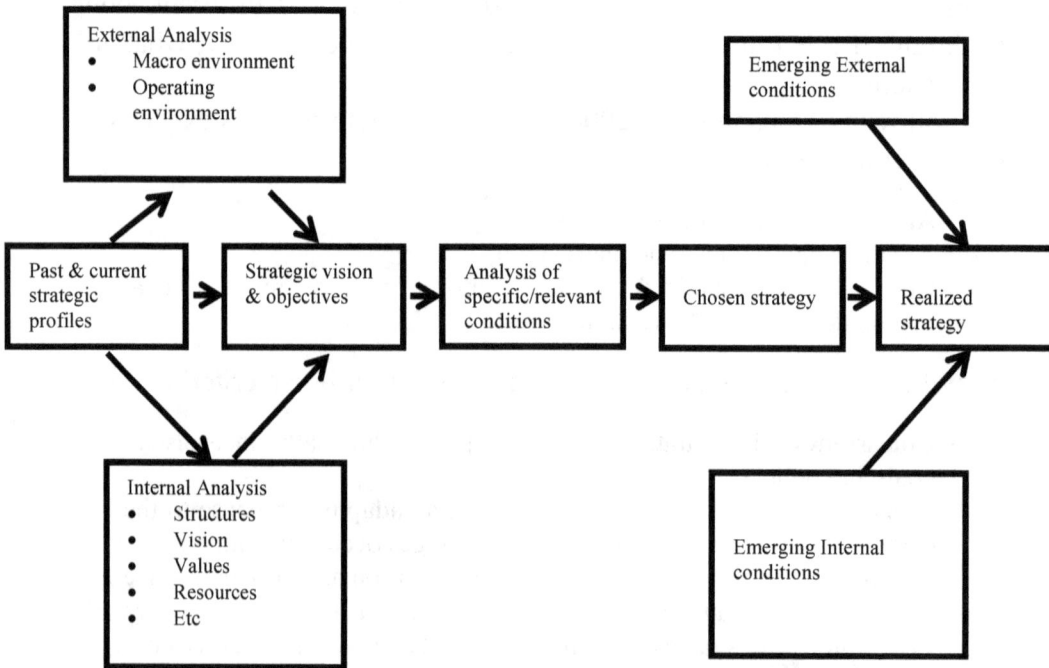

2.4 Evaluation of Strategies

Whether one subscribes to the planning perspective or the strategic management perspective, it is important to bear in mind that strategy can be neither formulated nor adjusted to changing circumstances without a process of strategy evaluation. Whether performed by an individual or as part of an organizational review procedure, strategy evaluation forms an essential step in the process of guiding an organization. In general terms, the process throws light on the efficiency and effectiveness of the comprehensive plans in achieving the desired results.

The process of Strategy Evaluation consists of following steps:

1. **Specifying Performance Benchmark** - Benchmarking is the process of comparing one's business processes and performance with the best performance within an industry. It helps management to identify industry leadership performance targets. Alternatively, the company can decide on its own internal performance benchmark against which the success or failure of the strategy can be evaluated.

   When fixing the benchmark performance target, it is essential to discover the special requirements for performing the main tasks outlined in the strategy and the capabilities (including resources) to perform these tasks. The performance indicators that best identify and express the special requirements might then be determined to be used for evaluation. The organization can use both quantitative and qualitative criteria for comprehensive assessment of performance. Quantitative criteria may include determination of net profit, ROI, earning per share, cost of production, rate of employee turnover etc. Among the qualitative factors are subjective evaluation of factors such as - skills and competencies, risk taking potential, flexibility etc.

2. **Measurement of Performance** - The actual performance is then compared with the benchmark targets. In doing the performance measurement, the strategists must specify the degree of tolerance limits between which variance between actual and target performance may be accepted.

3. **Analyzing Variance** – If the analysis reveals gaps in the company's performance, it is important to analyse the variance – i.e. seek good explanations for the differences. The explanations may be found in changes in either the internal or the external environments. The positive deviation indicates a better performance but it is quite

41

unusual exceeding the target always. The negative deviation is an issue of concern because it indicates a shortfall in performance. It is possible that negative deviations are simply due to overoptimistic targets in the first place.

4. **Taking Corrective Action** – Corrective actions must be planned and taken to close the gap between actual performance and the targets. In situations where the performance is consistently less than the desired performance, the management may be required to carry a detailed analysis of the factors responsible for such performance. If it happens that strategic goals have been too high, it may make sense to lower the targets.

It is often argued that the critical factors that impact performance may not be directly observable or may take long time to be noticed. By the time they become noticeable it may well be too late for an effective response. Thus, it is important for managers to look beyond the obvious facts regarding the short-term performance of a business when they evaluate the effectiveness of their strategies. They must appraise instead those more fundamental factors and trends that govern success in the long run. In this way, they are more likely to capture the hidden influencing factors in good time.

2.5 The military Analogy of Strategic Marketing

The marketing literature is excited about military analogies. The military origin of the concept of strategy seems to justify parallels that scholars draw between business and warfare, and encourage them to apply the principles of military strategy to business situations. Competing companies are considered enemies and market spaces are seen as war zones. Companies are therefore advised to probe opponents' weaknesses and design strategies that force them to stretch their resources. It is also considered strategically rewarding to concentrate a company's resources to attack an "enemy's" exposed position; fend off attacks from new entrants into a market; establish a position of dominance in certain markets; withdraw from certain markets or market segments; re-group resources and launch new assaults when appropriate in order to inflict devastating casualties. The military analogy reminds one of the need to combine strategic planning and flexible adaptation to achieve the most efficient and effective

42

outcomes of marketing efforts. A summary of the strategic options are presented in box 2.1 for a quick overview.

2.5.1 Attacking Strategies

They include frontal attacks, flank attacks, encirclements, bypass attacks and guerrilla attacks. In frontal attacks, the challenger matches the main competitor's product, advertising, price and distribution. There may be modified versions of this attack, using different marketing mix strategies. But the main message to customers is that the challenger's products and services fully match those of the leading competitor.

In using flank attack, the challenger identifies the leading competitor's weak spots and attacks them with a combination of marketing mix strategies. For example, the challenger may identify the competitor's products that are underperforming and offer similar products with better value propositions.

The encirclement maneuver is an attempt to capture a wide slice of the competitor's market share through a "blitz". It involves launching a grand offensive on several fronts – product, price, promotion and distribution. Encirclement makes sense when the challenger commands superior resources and believes a swift encirclement will break the opponent's will.

Strategies such as diversifying into unrelated product, diversifying into new geographic markets, and/or leapfrogging into new technologies to supplant existing products are labelled bypass attacks. When the challenger uses selective price cuts, intense promotional blitzes, and innovative distribution strategies to irritate the main competitor, these are described as guerrilla attacks. Normally guerrilla warfare is practiced by smaller firm against a larger one.

2.5.2 Defensive Strategies

They include preemptive strikes, position defence and leapfrogging (see box 2.1). These types of strategies are supposed to work best when they take place before the challenger makes an investment in the industry, or if they enter the industry before exit barriers are raised, making it difficult for the challenger to leave the industry. For this reason, an incumbent needs to take timely action to discourage a challenger from making any substantial commitment, because once the commitment is made, it is more difficult to dissuade the challenger from following through with the attack especially if exit barriers are high. If an attack has already begun, a defending company may attempt to lower its intensity and potential for harm, by directing the attack to areas where the company is less vulnerable, or in areas which are less desirable to the attacker (Porter, 1985). Or they should initiate actions designed to make the entrant's life difficult after entry has occurred. This may convince the entrant that its calculations were too optimistic.

Box2.1
Marketing Strategies in Military Language

1.   *Offensive marketing warfare strategies*
These may involve attacking market leaders   and runner-ups through frontal attack – i.e. a direct head-on confrontation with the market leader. A company may choose flanking attack (i.e. attacking the market leader's weaknesses) in order to minimize resource usage.

2.   *Defensive marketing warfare strategies*
They allow companies to defend their competitive advantages or lessen risk of being attacked, decrease effects of attacks.

3.   *Pre-emptive strikes*
These may be adopted when the company's analysis reveals that an attack from a competitor is eminent. The company may choose to attack before it is attacked. This may be through lowering prices in anticipation that a major competitor may lower its prices for a given product or service.

4.   *Position Defence*
This involves erection of fortifications. It may also take the form of directing the attack to areas where the company is less vulnerable, or in areas which are less desirable to the attacker.

5.   *Counter-offensives*
This strategy is recommended for companies that are under attack. They are to launch a counter-offensive at the attacker's weak point.

6.   *Guerrilla marketing warfare strategies*
These involve the art of attacking, retreating, hiding, then attacking again. The process is repeated until the competitor moves on to other markets.

7.   *Leapfrog strategy*
This involves avoiding confrontation by bypassing the enemy.

2.6 Summary

Strategic decisions taken by managers within an enterprise constitutes the organizing framework for all other functional decisions and activities. They also play a key role in a company's overall performance. Companies usually adopt a combination of planning and logically incremental/emergent approaches to strategy formulation and implementation. Planning allows them to adopt a systematic approach to decision making and performance measurement – providing employees with a clear growth path to follow. Emergent approaches encourage flexibility and adaptation to changes within and outside the company.

References

Bob de Wit and Ron Meyer (2004) *Strategy – An International Perspective* 3rd Edition (London, Thompson Books)

Dobson, Paul W., Starkey, Ken and Richards, John (2004) *Strategic Management: Issues and Cases*, 2nd Edition (Oxford; Wiley-Blackwell) Available at http://www.blackwellpublishing.com/content/bpl_images/content_store/sample_chapter/140511181x /dobson_str ategic%20management_sample%20chapter.pdf

Kay, J. (1993) *Foundations of Corporate Success: How Business Strategies Add Value.* New York: Oxford University Press.

Miller, P. (1991) "Strategic Human Resource Management: An assessment of progress". *Human Resource Management Journal*, 1(4): 23–39.

Mintzberg, H. and J. A. Waters (1982) "Tracking Strategy in an Entrepreneurial Firm" *Academy of Management Journal*, pp. 465-499.

Mintzberg, H. and J. A. Waters (1985) "Of Strategies Deliberate and Emergent" *Strategic Management Journal* (6): 257-272.

For Further Readings

Kumar, V. and J. Andrew Petersen (2005) "Using a Customer-Level Marketing Strategy to Enhance Firm Performance: A Review of

Theoretical and Empirical Evidence," *Journal of the Academy of Marketing Science*, 33/4 pp: 504-19.

Montgomery, Cynthia A., (2008) "Putting Leadership Back into Strategy," *Harvard Business Review* (January) pp: 54-60. www.hbr.org

Pascale, R.T. (1984) "Perspectives on Strategy: The Real Story Behind Honda's Success" *California Management Review* Vol. 26, No. 3 pp: 47-72

CHAPTER THREE

Rational Approaches to Market Knowledge Acquisition

3.1 Introduction

The planning approach to strategic decisions discussed in chapter two endorses rational decision making process in companies. This requires that managers conscientiously cultivate the intellectual habits of objectivity, explicitness, and clarity in their analysis of management issues. This approach enables decision makers to go beyond the limits of experience and base their decisions on what they consider to be sufficient information. In terms of marketing, this approach implies that marketing intelligence acquisition should provide an overall platform for all marketing activities. By systematically defining, assessing, and optimizing potential marketing opportunities within the context of available resources and core know how of a company, managers are able to develop and deliver products and services that customers really demand. This perspective invites an enquiry into the concept of knowledge as it applies in management studies. It also requires some insight into available procedures for systematic acquisition and analysis of information required for knowledge generation and dissemination within business organizations. The aim of this chapter is to provide such an insight.

The chapter starts with a presentation of a general framework for rational problem solving that scholars expect organizations and their managers to adopt. It then continues with a broad discussion of the concept of learning and knowledge acquisition, drawing mainly on the existing literature on organisational learning and knowledge management. This discussion provides a background for the introduction of an integrated conceptual framework that offers an overview of the key variables in a market knowledge development process. These variables include the types of knowledge, levels of knowledge development, the location of knowledge and the modes of knowledge development. Each set of variables is then discussed in details. The last section of the chapter discusses the implication of the contemporary understanding of knowledge and learning for market analysis and marketing strategy formulation.

3.2 A General Framework for Rational Decision Making

I have earlier argued that marketing managers are normally preoccupied with making decisions that help accomplish the following four major tasks in business organizations:

1. Assessing and understanding customer needs and expectations
2. Creating customer values based on this understanding.
3. Delivering the values so created in a manner that fulfils customer expectations and are superior to similar values created by competing companies.
4. Communicating the values to current and potential customers and other stakeholders.

Strategic planning scholars recommend that executives adopt a rational approach to decisions relating to the accomplishment of these tasks. The justification for their recommendation derives partly from the mistakes that managers are prone to make when they base their decisions only on experiences, intuition and "common sense". Rational decision making procedures allow them to deal with complex problems systematically in a step-wise fashion, with each step made explicit and examined separately as a comprehensible part of the whole.

As shown in Figure 3.1, most management scholars agree that rational decision making requires an initial awareness of a problem. Poorly formulated or wrongly understood problem may result in irrelevant studies and waste of resources. Furthermore, without problem identification the decision maker will not be able to determine what options are available to him. Problems must be seen in terms of the objectives that the decision maker has – i.e. something becomes a management problem if that thing constrains the attainment of the overall objectives of a company. Having identified the problem, the decision maker must agree on a set of criteria that captures the most important aspects of the problem. He then collects sufficient

48

information to examine the options available to him to solve the problem and the relative merits of these options (evaluated against the set of criteria). This is referred to as analysis. The analysis also entails the assessment of the risks and uncertainties related to the different alternatives (e.g. with regard to resource availability). At this stage the decision maker has to make a choice based on his assessment of the various options. This is followed by detailed planning on the steps to take to implement the decision. The plan becomes the road map and the milestones that management must be mindful about the implementation process. The evaluation is needed to see how it fits in with the changes that occur in the internal and external environment and to assess the accuracy of the forecasts they contain. Evaluation also focuses attention on deviations that may be in the design phase of the strategy or in the process of implementing the strategy.

In terms of this model, it is clear that the first responsibility of any marketing analyst is to help management define the key problems to be addressed. The problem may appear in the form of symptoms, e.g. declining sales of a particular product in a particular market segment in a given country. Dialogue with management helps clarify the nature of the problem. The process of market analysis therefore describes the distinct yet interrelated phases through which researchers go in their investigations. The execution of the various phases systematically brings the analysts through the activities required to achieve the overall goal of providing their clients with the information they need for their decision making purposes. Each phase consists of a combination of interrelated tasks and procedures.

The systematic approach to problem solving also helps businesses to learn and strengthen their internal capacities to adopt innovative approaches to the challenges that confront them in their operational environments. Individuals change knowledge base through the process and improve their frames of reference for the interpretation of their environments and experiences. The interpretation helps people build models of understanding and conceptual schemes that enable them to make sense of any new information they acquire. At company level, employees' interpretations of their experience help them improve existing operational skills and routines and even challenge the assumptions underlying existing routines within the company, a practice referred to as double loop learning in the organisational learning literature (Argyris and Schön, 1978). These processes of knowledge generation feed back into the company's stock of knowledge or organisational memory and constitute references for future investigation and decision making.

Learning thus requires deliberate efforts of individual employees with the support of top management. Without deliberate strategies to learn, organisations may remain inefficient. Reasons why employees may leave inefficiencies unquestioned in the first place can be traced to the organisational culture and the defensive routines it encourages. It has been argued that managers often remain prisoners of their conceptual frameworks (Hedberg, 1981). That is, they exhibit a general reluctance to leave old ways of thinking for new ones even though the old ones have been recognised as ineffective. The reluctance may be due partly to the desire to protect the ego of key managers in organisations who have supported the prevailing framework. It may also be due to the anxieties produced by prospects of change or to communication bottlenecks, rigid organisational structures as well as persistence of some myths within the organisations.

Figure 3.1 An Executive Decision Making Framework

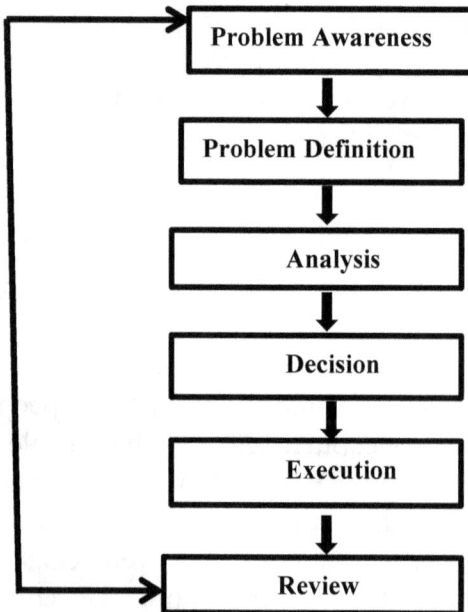

3.3   The Concept of Knowledge and Learning in Marketing

There is a general agreement among marketing scholars that market information and knowledge is crucial to an effective management of a company. Managers need to identify current and emergent customer needs and gain insight into marketing activities needed to fulfil these needs. They also need to acquire information about strategies that immediate competitors pursue or are likely to pursue in given markets. The more complex the operational environment is the more critical market information becomes for successful business operations. Thus, Kohli and Jaworski (1990:6) define marketing management to embrace "the organisation-wide generation of market intelligence, dissemination of this intelligence across departments and organisation-wide responsiveness to it". That is, market-oriented companies are expected to gather, interpret and use market information in a more systematic, thoughtful and anticipatory manner than less market-oriented companies. These scholars, therefore, see market orientation in terms of functional activities that specific units of organizations perform (Lafferty and Hult, 2001).

Market orientation scholars have extensively studied the link between the degree of market orientation of companies and their business performance. The general understanding produced by these studies is that the greater the level of market orientation of a company the higher its performance would be. This has strengthened marketing scholars' conviction in the fundamental role of market knowledge generation and dissemination in overall business strategy formulation and implementation. By expanding the type of information collected about current and prospective customers and increasing the number of people who have access to the information, companies are able to base their customer-oriented marketing strategies on solid and reliable knowledge about those they intend to serve.

In business-to-business marketing situations, customer-oriented dispositions of vendors would require them to acquire information covering issues such as the number and profile of key employees of their customers, technology used, parent or subsidiary company details, competitor information, and the latest news and analyst reports on customers and competitors operating within the industry. In addition to customer-based information, factors such as government regulations and competition that influence the needs and preferences of a company's customers must be monitored. Furthermore, the generation of market intelligence must rely not only on customer surveys, but also on a range of complementary mechanisms. For example, informal discussion with trade partners and distributors can be a good source of customer information.

Customer knowledge dissemination component of market orientation involves ensuring vertical and horizontal flows of communication within and between departments. This may be done through the establishment of database on customers (covering the expressed needs as well as satisfactions and complaints about current products and services offered), the circulation of periodic newsletters, formal meetings, and informal story telling.

3.3.1 The Learning Process

Since organisational success depends on the appropriate and smooth dissemination procedure, all departments and employees of an organisation should understand the importance of the effective use of disseminated information and create a favourable climate for using this information through inter-functional coordination (Narver and Slater, 1990).

Some organizational learning researchers argue that organisations learn only through their members. Cohen and Levinthal (1990) suggest that cognitive structures of individuals provide the grounding for organisational learning. For Senge (1990), an enterprise cannot learn unless its members modify their mental models so as to integrate the complexity of the organisation's functioning. They do so either by benefiting from the knowledge acquired by the existing members or by recruiting new members who bring with them knowledge that the organisation did not previously have (Simon, 1991).

The motivation for an individual learning comes from the detection of a mismatch between the individual's current behaviour and his expected outcomes. The desire to improve an individual's outcomes may be either intrinsically generated (i.e. self-awareness) or extrinsically triggered. In either case, the effectiveness of learning is expected to be seen in individual and/or organizational performance. That is, even if learning may not immediately translate into performance enhancement, the expectations of performance benefits encourage individuals and organisations to engage in further learning activities.

The more varied interpretations are given to the information the greater the probability that they will result in changes in organisational behaviour as a whole. Re-interpretation entails the process of unlearning. Hedberg (1981) defines unlearning as a process through which learners discard obsolete and misleading knowledge, replacing them with new knowledge. Some writers therefore see unlearning as the first step in a learning process (Huber, 1991). But in terms of time, both unlearning and learning may take place concurrently.

The concept of unlearning can be further explained with reference to Argyris and Schön's (1978) distinction between *single loop learning* and *double loop learning*. Single loop learning refers to the conscious, intentional and rational activity undertaken by actors in an organisation to detect and correct discrepancies that appear between their expectations and the results produced by their actions. Correcting errors provides a learning experience that ensures that similar problems can be effectively addressed in the future. But if an employee who corrects the error were to ask himself "what in this organisation has prevented the workers from questioning practices that have resulted in the errors in the first place", he will be setting off a process leading to double loop learning (Argyris, 1994). Double loop learning therefore allows an organisation to change its current mindset and the direction of its actions and fortunes. In business organisations, this type of learning sustains the long-term competitive advantages of the business within its changing operational context.

Seen in terms of market analysis, it can be argued that companies act through their individual employees who perform specific functions. For example, sales people and service providers are in regular contact with customers, purchasing officers are in contact with suppliers, R&D staff in contact with other players within their industry etc. All these relationships produce rich sources of market knowledge that companies can tap. Thus, the international marketing literature shows a good appreciation of the importance of "people on the spot" in market knowledge generation in distant markets. Individuals embedded in the local environment are able to register errors of interpretation of ideas and thoughts that their companies may have, and rectify them quickly enough to avoid misunderstandings that may sow the seed of mistrust between companies.

3.3.2 Marketing Intelligence Generation

From the planning perspective, marketing decisions will framed around the following five tasks, or functions: (1) analysis of current marketing situation (2) defining marketing objectives, (3) assess marketing opportunities based on the analysis (4) formulating plans and developing marketing organizations and structures to achieve the objectives, (4) deciding on specific actions/tactics, (6) evaluating the process and instituting necessary control measures. This step-by-step approach enables management to systematically identify, evaluate, and rank potential marketing opportunities obtained systematically from many different sources.

When a marketing opportunity is selected for implementation and moved from a strategic portfolio to marketing operations, marketing managers need to collect a sufficient amount of relevant information to clearly determine whether or not a given marketing opportunity may be implemented in a timely and systematic fashion. Therefore, marketing managers need to develop a deep understanding of three fundamental elements of marketing activities—the dynamics of each market segment, consumers' purchase decisions, and consumers' levels of satisfaction. These three marketing activities account for the major portions of any marketing effort.

The process of collecting information and converting it into marketing intelligence is the responsibility of both the executives and marketing managers. Sources of marketing information are both external and internal. The external sources include the business environment, the marketplace, and the competitive climate. The internal sources are based on the marketing competencies and core knowledge accumulated among the executives and marketing managers of an enterprise.

It is important to remind ourselves that business knowledge decays due to the dynamism of the internal and external operational environments of companies. Since the validity of knowledge changes with context and time, a continuous process of knowledge creation and dissemination is necessary if managers are to forestall situations where companies are managed by a dominant logic for a long time without it being questioned.

3.4 A Conceptual Model of International Business Knowledge Analysis

Building on the discussions above, Figure 3.2 provides a conceptual framework for understanding market knowledge development process. It sees knowledge development from four main perspectives

1. Modes of knowledge development
2. Levels of knowledge
3. Location of knowledge
4. Types of knowledge

We have earlier noted that companies may obtain their market knowledge either by acquiring it or by reflecting and reinterpreting existing information in their internal data bank. This acquisition may happen through experimentation, surveys, formal interviews, conversations within informal and social networks, or through recruitment of people who have the knowledge. Regarding the levels of knowledge, we have argued earlier that knowledge can be found at individual levels of companies. Added to this, knowledge may be seen also at organisational, industry and community levels. In terms of location, we can draw a distinction between home country based knowledge, target country knowledge as well as regional market knowledge. All these classifications are discussed in details below.

Figure 3.2: A Conceptual Framework for International Market Knowledge Development

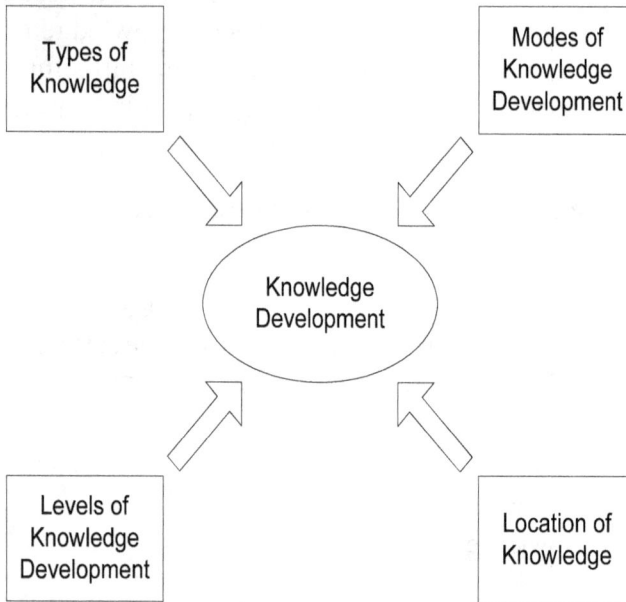

3.4.1 Types of Market Knowledge

We can distinguish between three sets of dichotomous characteristics that shape a company's market knowledge. These characteristics may also be seen as representing three continua. They are (1) individual-collective knowledge, (2) rational-emotional knowledge, and (3) tacit-explicit knowledge. Figure 3.3 provides a schematic illustration of the types of knowledge that combinations of these characteristics produce.

Figure 3.3 Continua of Market Knowledge

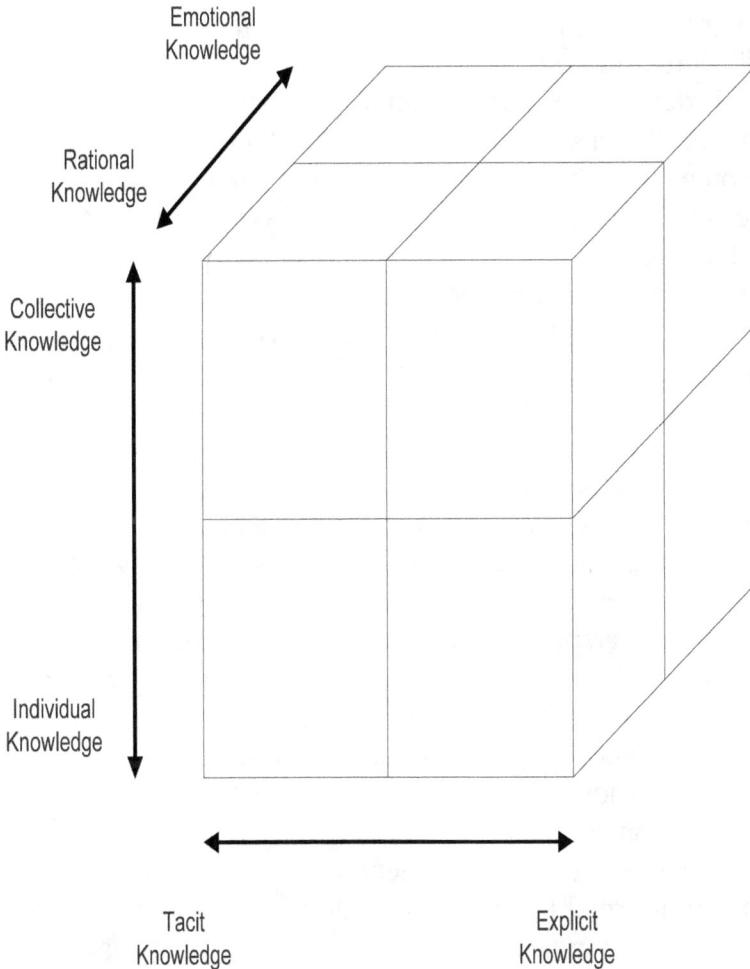

Tacit-Explicit Continuum

The concepts of tacit and explicit knowledge have been popularised by Polanyi (1966). Explicit knowledge describes the type of knowledge that is codified and transmittable in formal, systematic forms. Tacit knowledge is the opposite. It is hard to formalise and transmit since it is deeply embedded in people's actions and experiences of their lifeworld.

Two dimensions of tacit knowledge have been identified in the literature. The first is the cognitive dimension, which covers people's "mental models", beliefs and viewpoints that guide their action but are difficult to present in a logical manner and language. The second is the "technical" dimension, covering the individual's concrete know-how, skills and dexterity that enable him to perform a specific task in a unique manner. It is a summary construct explaining his capability as a worker. Some writers also refer to tacit knowledge as intuitive knowledge, while others consider it as an aspect of a person's wisdom or holistic knowledge.

Hitherto, the literature sees tacit and explicit knowledge as alternative categories of knowledge. Each category is presented in binary terms rather than in degrees. In practice, however, one can observe various combinations of explicit and tacit knowledge in the daily actions of people. That is, some forms of knowledge are not entirely tacit while others are entirely explicit. It is therefore purposeful to describe knowledge in terms of its degree of "tacitness" or "explicitness" and thus place this typology of knowledge on a continuum as illustrated in Figure 3.3.

Seen from the perspective of international market analysis, explicit knowledge would include understanding derived from statistical data analyses about economic, political, social, technological and legal aspects of the markets in specific countries or regions. It also includes specific product knowledge and all other kinds of market related knowledge that can be explicitly articulated. This kind of knowledge may be obtained from a wide variety of sources including surveys, interviews and informal conversations. On the other hand, tacit market knowledge would emerge from interactions with other players on the market. This type of knowledge represents people's interpretations of events and opinions of key influencers in given markets. These interpretations, as said earlier, are normally based on the experiences of individuals who have worked and/or lived in the focal markets.

Rational-Emotional Knowledge Continuum

The third force that shapes market knowledge is captured in the rational-emotional knowledge continuum. Conventional economic thinking endorses realism, i.e. the understanding that reality is objective and exists independent of the person perceiving it. Knowledge in this regard is also objective and devoid of sentiments and subjective dispositions. Contrary to this perspective, Kriger (1999) introduces the concept of emotional knowledge, arguing that some aspects of tacit knowledge are actually anchored in the emotions of people.

Interest in emotional knowledge has been growing rapidly in business organizations in recent years – both for purposes of internal organizational development (i.e. internal marketing) and for strengthening relationships with key customers. Business leaders are encouraged to find ways to energize themselves and their workers, to recoil to rooms of silence and to engage in meditation and self-reflection in order to sharpen their intuitive capabilities to make decisions that could change the fortune of their companies. Protagonists of emotional knowledge maintain that human energy is most effectively used when it supplements, not supplants, rational decision making techniques. In their view, contemporary rational models tend to ignore both the negative and positive human attributes in organizations. The negative attributes include greed, selfishness, manipulation, secrecy, distrust, anxiety, self-absorption, fear, burnout, and feelings of abuse that tend to derail organizational efforts. Positive attributes include appreciation, collaboration, virtuousness, vitality, and meaningfulness. Members of such organizations are characterized by trustworthiness, resilience, wisdom, and humility.

This awareness has led companies to use emotional appeals in their marketing strategies. Brand names and company logos are evident examples of symbolisation in marketing, allowing explicit product attributes and company identities to be communicated through emotional codes. The use of emotionally provocative advertising captions by Benetton is another very well documented example of symbolism in marketing. From this perspective, the concept of emotional knowledge is not strange to the marketing literature, although scholars have not explicitly applied the concept.

Apart from symbolism, explicit market knowledge can be converted into emotional knowledge for internal marketing purposes. This can be done by excitation, a process by which marketing strategies are legitimated and communicated to employees through the use of emotional appeals. For example, the plight of AIDS patients in the developing countries can be used by a pharmaceutical company as a justification for cost cutting and rationalisation policies within the company. By reducing cost the company may be able to sell AIDS drugs relatively cheaply and thereby save many lives in those parts of the world.

Along the same lines, intuitive/tacit market knowledge and vision of a CEO can be converted into emotional knowledge that would motivate employees to exhibit greater commitment, creativity and energy in the performance of their tasks. Similarly, certain groups of employees may harbour frustrations and strains at their work due to dissatisfactions with company policies and strategies. Such strains may derive from what may be termed their emotional knowledge. By offering them the opportunity to vent their frustrations, they are able to convert the emotional knowledge to explicit knowledge that management can deal with. The same holds true for customers whose complaints may contain elements of emotional strains due to poor service quality.

Mobilisation is a process similar to excitation. It involves the use of emotional language and tools to motivate employees to take actions on behalf of the organisation. In times of crisis a new CEO may have a burning desire to turn the organisation around. His determination may be based on his emotional energy and knowledge. But to succeed, he must share these emotions with his colleagues at the top as well as other employees of the organisation. This is done by mobilisation where his emotional knowledge is converted into tacit knowledge which is, in turn, communicated to the other organisational members.

3.4.2 Knowledge Levels

As noted above the knowledge levels include individual knowledge, group/team knowledge, organisational/industry level knowledge as well as social/cultural knowledge.

Individual Knowledge

When individuals are employed in a company, they arrive with a certain set of basic knowledge about the manner in which their jobs can be performed. This may be referred to as their personal background market knowledge. In the course of their duties they interact with their colleagues, discuss issues relevant to their work; agreeing with them on some of the issues disagreeing on others. This process of interaction produces group knowledge.

The term individual knowledge therefore refers to the repository of managers' basic "beliefs" and patterns of understanding that they bring to bear on their tasks and responsibilities within their organisations. This is usually combined with their cognitive capacity to synthesize and make personal sense of the in coming signals from the environment.

Group Knowledge

Through collective encounters members of a decision making group are offered the opportunity to discuss issues that are of concern to the group. This produces generally held, group-based understanding of the phenomenon and the emergence of norms that define expected and accepted behaviour by members of the group. This may be called group knowledge. The relative influence and contribution of individuals in the group to the group knowledge depends on the depth of their knowledge, their position in the organisational hierarchy and the decision-making tradition within the organisation. Group members argue, provide evidence to substantiate viewpoints, negotiate with those with dissenting views and use other forms of manipulative tactics to increase the influence of their knowledge over the decisions arrived at.

Organisational or Industry Knowledge

The personal experiences of the staff combine with group level understanding to provide inputs into the storehouse of the organisational knowledge. This storehouse may take the form of a data bank or the tacitly shared understanding of the company as a whole. It constitutes the organisational memory. This means every institution or organisation has its own body of transmitted knowledge that supplies its members with organisationally appropriate rules of conduct. Upon entering an organisation, a new member undergoes a process of socialization or cognitive reconstruction in order to acquire the stock of knowledge and orientation that is required to be an acceptable member of the organisation.

Cultural Knowledge

Cultural knowledge is the shared understandings which an individual acquires through socialization and interaction with people within a given society. They provide the fundamental basis for sense-making of the signals that filter into an individual's cognitive structure. These understandings provide what may be called standardized operating procedures, useful in handling repetitive situations. Cultural knowledge is therefore more broad-based than the organisational knowledge and its sources lie beyond the organisational boundaries.

3.4.3 Modes of Knowledge Transformation and Development

The term holistic knowledge may be used to describe the ability of employees to understand the interrelationship between various types of knowledge that are directly or indirectly used by organisational members within and outside the organisation. It makes sense to argue that top management must possess such holistic knowledge in order to effectively lead businesses within a dynamic global environment.

An important aspect of this holistic business knowledge is an understanding of the patterns of knowledge conversion and flow within organisations. Nonaka and Takeuchi's (1995) typology of patterns of knowledge conversion provided initial impetus to a stream of knowledge conversion studies within the knowledge research tradition. Previous writings have perceived knowledge conversion in organisations in a unidirectional mode i.e. from tacit to explicit forms of knowledge. Nonaka and Takeuchi (1995) argue in favour of bi-directional transformation and identify four different patterns of interaction between tacit and explicit knowledge. These are combination (from explicit to explicit), internalisation (from explicit to tacit), socialisation (from tacit to tacit), and externalisation (from tacit to explicit). Kriger (1999) argues that socialisation is an inappropriate description of the mode of transferring tacit knowledge to other people, since socialisation involves emotions as well. He therefore suggests role modelling as a more appropriate concept to describe tacit to tacit conversion. When emotional knowledge is added to the list of knowledge, the conversion framework has to be extended. Accordingly, he suggests five additional modes of knowledge conversion. These are interpretation (from emotional to explicit), mobilisation (from emotional to tacit), symbolisation (from explicit to emotional), and socialisation (from emotional to emotional). That is, socialisation entails appealing to emotions of individuals in an interactive process.

For the purposes of this book, the process of knowledge conversion describes the manner and extent to which various types of marketing knowledge can be disseminated within a company. Where market knowledge is obtained in the form of survey reports, it constitutes explicit knowledge. Following Nonaka and Takeuchi (1995) this type of knowledge can be disseminated within a company in either or both of two ways; combination and internalisation. Combination is the typical rational and logical mode of communicating new knowledge within Western societies and businesses. The understanding here is that new knowledge is created not merely through the addition of new information to the existing body of information but through the reconfiguration of existing information, i.e. sorting, re-categorisation and/or exploring alternative logically appropriate interpretations of existing body of knowledge. Meetings are usually held and the report is presented and discussed, using other known concepts and systems to interpret and understand its meanings. In other words, the reflection and understanding process takes the form of combining and systematising the new knowledge with existing vocabulary, frameworks and models. The outcome of the deliberations is communicated further to those who were not at the meeting via computer networks, telephones, small talks and other meetings.

Internalisation involves the conversion of explicit to tacit knowledge. This is actually the crux of the dissemination and provides an indication of the extent to which the knowledge would actually be applied in the concrete actions of the company's employees. In simple terms, it is a process of learning by doing. If the knowledge provided in the market report is effectively internalised, all employees would integrate the ideas into their daily behaviour. If not, the report may produce limited impact on the organisation. Such forms of knowledge conversion are context-dependent. That is, they are dependent on intimate knowledge of situations in which they apply rather than an understanding of abstract rules. The idea here is that groups of individuals, e.g. (a team of marketers) who visit the same group of customers in a given country or regional market, engage in common experiences. Through group reflections they tend to acquire a shared understanding of these experiences and this constitutes a tacit knowledge for them. As and when individuals in this team interact with other organisational members, their experiences are re-shared and new reflections are engaged in. The interaction may result in modification of earlier interpretations of the experience. The tacit knowledge created at this stage is shared by a wider group within the organisation than those who initially are engaged in the experience.

Knowledge obtained through this means may, over time, develop into routines and take-for-granted actions if not frequently reflected on. In this regard, the knowledge so obtained can hold the danger of constraining organisational capabilities to critically perceive market situations and act differently.

A typical example of dissemination of explicit market knowledge through internalisation or practice is the manner in which companies may handle customers' complaints or requests. A key customer may send a complaint to a vendor and request prompt actions to be taken. Some companies may designate specific units or employees to handle such complaints or requests. In recent years, however, an increasing number of companies have established computer aided networks or so called "answer centres" to process the complaints and questions on 24 hour basis. The idea is that the speed with which the customer receives response to his requests would provide him or her with high level of satisfaction and thereby loyalty to the companies having such facilities. Kriger (1999), however, cautions about an over-reliance on computer systems to attend to customer requests and complaints. His argument is that there are emotional components attached to customers' contacts with their vendors and such emotional elements cannot be handled by artificial intelligence systems such as "answer centres". Customers therefore become frustrated in their contact with companies that use the computer as a reliable interface.

3.5 Summary

Most managers are keenly aware of the role that knowledge plays in the attainment of their organizational objectives. Knowledge of the needs of stakeholders facilitates decision-making capabilities as well as the learning processes in organizations. Without knowledge and deliberate strategies to learn, organisations may remain inefficient. Knowledge also stimulates cultural change and innovation. For this reason all well-managed businesses seek access to an extensive pool of knowledge. Thus, the way organizations gather, share and exploit knowledge can be central to their ability to develop successfully. The literature has developed different classifications of knowledge to help organizations identify and manage their pools of knowledge. Some of the classifications identify individual-collective knowledge, rational-emotional knowledge, and tacit-explicit knowledge. There are also models of dissemination and conversion of the different types of knowledge at different levels of an organization. A good understanding of these models helps managers in their knowledge management endeavours.

References

Argyris, Chris and Schön, Donald (1978) *Organizational learning: A Theory of Action Perspective* (Reading, MA: Addison Wesley)

Argyris, Chris (1994) *Knowledge for Action* (San Francisco CA, Jossey-Bass)

Cohen, Westley M., and Levinthal, Daniel A. (1990), "Absorptive Capacity: A New Perspective on Learning and Innovation", *Administrative Science Quarterly*, 35: 128-152

Hedberg, B (1981) "How organizations lean and unlearn" in Nystrom, P.C. and Starbuck, W.J. (Eds.), *Handbook of organizational design*. (London, Oxford University Press) pp: 3-27

Huber, George P. (1991), "Organizational Learning: The Contributing Processes and the Literatures." *Organization Science* Vol. 2 No. 1 pp: 88-115

Kohli, A.K., and Jaworski, B.J (1990) "Market Orientation: The Construct, Research Propositions and Managerial Implications" *Journal of Marketing* Vol. 54, April pp. 1-18

Kriger, M.P. (1999) "The Many Ways of Knowing: Implications for the Research and Teaching of Knowledge." Presented at the international conference *Re-Organizing Knowledge: Trans-forming Institutions*, University of Massachusetts, Amherst, MA,

Lafferty, B.A., and G.T.M. Hult, (2001) "A synthesis of contemporary market orientation perspectives" *European Journal of Marketing* Vol. 35 No. 1, 92-109

Narver, John C. and Slater, Stanley F., (1990) "The Effect of Market Orientation on Business Profitability" *Journal of Marketing*, Vol. 54 October pp. 20-35

Nonaka, I., Takeuchi, H. (1995). *The Knowledge- Creating Company* (New York-Oxford, Oxford University Press)

Polanyi, M., (1966) *The Tacit Dimension* (London, Routledge and Kegan Paul)

Senge, P.M. (1990): *The Fifth Discipline,* (New York, Doubleday).

Simon, H.A. (1991) "Bounded Rationality and Organisational Learning" *Organisation Science* 2: 125-134

For Further Readings

Feldman, M.S. and March, J.G., (1981) "Information in Organizations as Signal and Symbol" *Administrative Science Quarterly* 26, pp.171-186

Nonaka, Ikujiro and Johansson, J., (1985) "Japanese Management: What about the 'Hard' Skills?" *Academy of Management Review*, Vol. 10, no. 2 pp: 181-191

Nonaka, Ikujiro. (1994) "A Dynamic Theory of Organisational Knowledge Creation" *Organisation Science* Vol. 5 No. 1 pp 14-37

Salaman, G., and Butler, J., (1990) "Why Managers Won't Learn" *Management Education and Development* Vol. 21 No. 3 pp: 183-191

Sitkin, S. B. (1996). "Learning through failure: The strategy of small losses" In M. Cohen and U. Sproull (Eds.), *Organizational learning* Thousand Oaks, CA: Sage. pp. 541–577.

CHAPTER FOUR

A Framework for Market Opportunity Analysis

4.1 Introduction

Chapter 3 introduces the reader to general approach to rational decision making and the role of knowledge generation in the process. It also discusses the concept of knowledge and different types of knowledge and how knowledge can be transformed and disseminated in organizations. This chapter builds on these previous discussions and guides the analyst in systematizing his/her data collection process. In specific terms, the chapter introduces the reader to an integrated model for market opportunity analysis in any given country. This model identifies three key dimensions that a market analyst must be concerned about in any specific analysis: *(1) the size of the potential market, (2) the marketing efforts required to serve the customers effectively, and (3) the extent to which customers are satisfied with the current marketing efforts of key competitors.* Furthermore, the model suggests five main sources of data for making assessments in these three areas. The chapter also provides an overview of arithmetic formulae that market analysts may use in estimating the market potentials of their (client) companies.

4.2 Dimensions of Market Opportunity Analysis

A marketing executive's first concern is to determine the potential size of demand in a given market, since market size is an important indication of potential revenue. But the potential demand must be examined against the background of competition or potential competition in the market. If a market is relatively large but is already effectively served by competitors, it offers a new entrant no substantial opportunity in the short run. In other words, market opportunity depends not only on the size of potential demand but also on how well that demand is already served by other companies, foreign or local.

Even where competition is less effective, it is important to assess the marketing efforts that may be required to serve the potential consumers effectively. This assessment enables the company to determine whether it can make profit by entering the market and is prepared to commit the required resources to the development of the market. The following three key determinants of foreign market opportunity are worth the attention of every market analyst. They constitute the primary outcomes of a market opportunity analysis.

- Size of market.
- Marketing programme requirement to satisfy market wants.
- Quality of competitors' marketing strategies.

In order to gain a detailed knowledge of these three determinants of market opportunity, a market analyst is required to conduct five separate analyses from which he can obtain the information he needs. Let us call them components of a market opportunity analysis. These are:

- Demand Analysis
- Segmentation Analysis
- Industry Analysis
- Competitor Analysis
- Channel Analysis

Figure 4.1 provides an overview of the relationship between the various analyses that provide answers to the key questions of market size, marketing programme requirements and competitors' current marketing strategies. The understanding here is that each analysis generates information that provides a partial insight into the issues. The information collected through each analysis is then brought together and critically examined for consistency. Through this process, the investigator gains a more qualified insight into the issues under investigation.

4.2.1 Assessment of Market Size

A market may be defined as a group of people or companies able and willing to buy a product or service to fulfil a given purpose, either production or consumption. This definition emphasises the point that a market is comprised of *final buyers* of a product or service rather than *intermediate buyers* (i.e. those buying only for resale of the product). From a short-term perspective, a market may be said to exist for a given product or services only when there is demand for it. Demand here refers to need backed by purchasing power. That is, the presence of an unfulfilled want among some group of people constitutes an *incipient demand*, but not an immediate market to a company (various types of demand are discussed below). The concern of most market analysts is to assess market demand that a company's products can immediately satisfy.

Kotler (1994: 247) defines *market demand* for a product as "the total volume (of the product) that would be bought by a defined customer group in a defined geographical area in a defined marketing environment under a defined marketing programme". From this definition we note that total market demand is not a fixed number but a function of stated conditions, i.e. the characteristics of the customer group, the geographical area, the period of time as well as market environmental considerations and the marketing programme that the company is prepared to develop for the market.

Fig. 4.1   **A DESCRIPTIVE FRAMEWORK FOR INTERNATIONAL MARKET OPPORTUNITY ANALYSIS**

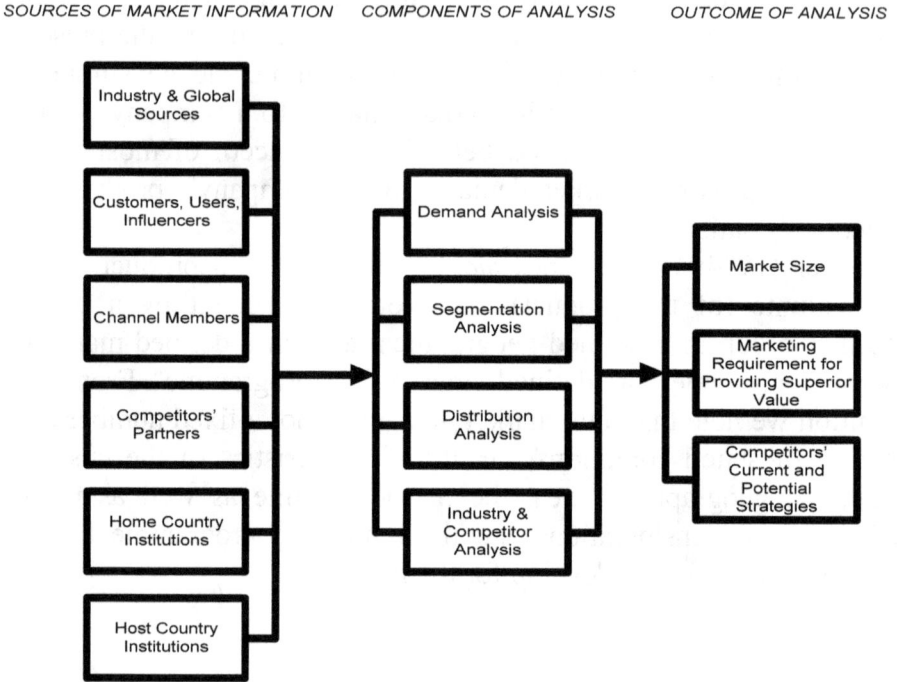

SOURCES OF MARKET INFORMATION   COMPONENTS OF ANALYSIS   OUTCOME OF ANALYSIS

Industry & Global Sources

Customers, Users, Influencers

Channel Members

Competitors' Partners

Home Country Institutions

Host Country Institutions

Demand Analysis

Segmentation Analysis

Distribution Analysis

Industry & Competitor Analysis

Market Size

Marketing Requirement for Providing Superior Value

Competitors' Current and Potential Strategies

Source: Kuada (2008)

Detailed market size analysis is of primary importance in the final screening process. If the market size is too small, the company may consider discarding the market on the basis of size. But some companies may decide to enter a relatively small market if they consider it to have substantial long-term prospects. A company may, for example, apply a rule-of-thumb decision criterion saying that if potential sales are less than $250,000 a year the market may be discarded. Market size must be considered in relation to the profit margin to be expected. For example a market of $250,000 a year with a 50% margin will be more attractive than a $500,000 market with only 20% margin.

Another dimension to consider is the turnover rate of the client company's investment. A small market with a faster turnover will generate a higher return on investment than a bigger market with a slower turnover. Assume total sales of the product is $250,000 in country **A** and $500,000 in country **B**. Assume further that the margins in countries **A** and **B** are 50% and 25% respectively. In absolute terms the margins are $125,000 in both countries. But since the investment in country **B** is twice your investment in country **A**, the returns on investment in country **A** are better.

4.2.2   Types of Demand

A key consideration in new market opportunity assessment is the estimation of the size of demand. Market demand measurement calls for a clear understanding of the market involved. Various classificatory models have been presented in marketing textbooks to help analysts in gaining insights into the nature of the markets of interest to them. Analysts are usually advised to start their demand measurement with an assessment of the potential market for their products in a given country or industry. The *potential market* for a product or service is the set of customers who have shown some level of interest in the product. This is different from the *available market,* which is the set of customers who not only have the need for the product or service but also the income to acquire it.

A distinction is also drawn between the target market and the penetrated market. The label *"target market"* is used to describe that part of the available market that the company is interested in serving and the *penetrated* market is the set of buyers/ users who have already bought the product. Vendors can therefore only target the "unpenetrated" part of the target market or encourage the users in the "penetrated" segment to intensify that usage and thereby increase their volume of purchase.

As hinted above, there are various categories of demand that can be of interest to a company and to which its strategy can be directed. Toyne and Walter (1989) provide another useful classification of demand. They suggest that market analysts must be mindful of the following three categories of demand:

- Incipient demand
- Latent demand
- Current demand.

Incipient market demand is demand that is expected to exist in the future. For example if the people in a specific country are aware of a particular need or want, but their level of income is insufficient to satisfy it, their needs then constitute incipient market demand. This holds true for certain categories of products in developing and transitional economies. Large companies nurture incipient demand either through the development of cheaper variants of the products that the consumers need or by establishing an awareness of the company through social development activities. This gives them a competitive leverage when the level of income in the society increases to the extent that consumers could buy the products.

Latent market demand represents an untapped demand. This is the case where a demand exists for a particular product or service, but no company has discovered it and therefore has not offered the consumers the desired products or services. It could also represent demand that has been stifled as a result of government regulations. If the regulations are changed, the demand becomes manifest. For example, Cubans have been disallowed to own mobile phones until 2008, when government regulations were changed to allow their purchase and possession.

Existing market demand is what consumers (in a given country or community) are prepared to pay for. It can be higher than the level of current consumption, including that proportion of demand not as yet satisfied by currently available products due to imperfections in the marketing system.

A great deal of market research that analysts conduct focus attention on existing market demand, few are aware of latent market demand and nearly all ignore incipient demand. But for large companies selling standardised products on a global market, awareness of incipient demand is important for continued growth. Thus companies such as Coca Cola and Pepsi Cola design long term strategies that anticipate demand for their products in remote parts of the world by establishing their names and images in those societies long before the citizens are capable of buying the products.

4.2.3 Assessment of Marketing Programme Requirements

Each company believes that its products have unique attributes compared to competitors' products. It is management's task to communicate these product characteristics to potential customers in a manner that encourages them to adopt the product. Decision to adopt may also be influenced by prices and product delivery conditions. These considerations form part of the company's marketing strategy. This part of the analysis requires a close collaboration with the management of the client company who understands the company's overall business plan and therefore knows what the company may be willing to do and how much resource it may be willing to commit to the marketing effort. The analyst can, however, conceptualise the marketing programmes in terms of the following 3Ps:

Promises: These include what the company should promise prospective customers in its marketing package. They relate to product features (possible collaboration in the product design in the case of technology), prices, payment conditions, delivery plans, service commitments etc. Promises should meet or even surpass the marketing requirements of target customers as revealed in the market analyses.

Processes: This covers plans for how to communicate these values to prospective customers, how to canvas for orders and how to organise the marketing activities (this is part of the communication parameters in the marketing mix strategy).

Providers: This covers the organisation of the marketing process – i.e. who should do what in the value creation and delivery process, at what stages and at what cost.

4.2.3 Assessment of Competitors' Marketing Strategy

The marketing literature provides guides on how this type of assessment can be undertaken. Since competitors themselves are naturally unwilling to reveal what they are doing and how customers' assess their performance, the analyst would have to obtain the information indirectly by using a combination of sources. As we can see subsequently, one important source of such information is segmentation analysis. Analyzing each competitor's performance within the context of a specific segment would allow the analyst to focus on the specific types of customers that each competitor has satisfied. It also helps identify groups of customers that are likely to be persuaded to switch from the competitors' products and services to those offered by the company.

Such information could be obtained through scanning major industry news periodicals for news about customers and consumer organisations' reactions to events in which competitors have been involved. Furthermore, primary data can be collected from customers and channel members about key competitors as part of the general market data collection.

4.3 Components of Market Opportunity Analysis

4.3.1 Segmentation Analysis

The aggregate demand analysis by itself cannot determine whether a company can establish a sufficiently profitable niche in the aggregate market to warrant taking advantage of the opportunity. This requires a segmentation analysis. Market segmentation entails the division of a heterogeneous mass market into a number of distinct categories. The aim of segmentation analysis is therefore to identify and describe segments of buyers who would respond similarly to marketing programme alternatives.

Segmentation analysis usually ends up with the selection of which segments to serve. The selected market segment then constitutes the company's target market. Some attractiveness criteria to be considered in evaluating a market segment are:

- The market growth potential.
- The level of market domination by large and powerful competitors.
- The entry barriers and the prospects of being able to attain and maintain a certain "critical mass" (i.e. a significant size of segments) to be an efficient exporter to that market.

Contrary to popular expectations, market segmentation is not always easy. It is particularly a difficult task to conduct a meaningful segmentation of industrial markets. Often the same industrial products have multiple applications and several products can be used in the same application.

There are two major approaches to market segmentation. The first is *a priori* approach in which the segmentation variables and their categories are decided before data are collected. The second approach is a clustering-based segmentation design in which the segments are determined *a posteriori,* for example through the use of cluster analysis of relevant variables.

Taking the a priori approach first, industrial markets can be meaningfully segmented using the following criteria:

- Demographic characteristics, including the nature of the industry, the sizes of the companies and their location.
- Operating variables, including company technology, nature of products, customer capabilities (i.e. technical, financial and operational)
- Purchasing approaches, i.e. the manner in which they organise their purchasing process, the power structures that characterise the purchase decision making units and their policies and attitudes to vendor-customer relationship.
- Situational factors, including the urgency of order fulfillment, product application, and the size of order.

With regard to *a posteriori* segmentation, Day (1990) identifies four response profiles: application or usage situation benefit sought or derived sensitivity to marketing variables, and purchase behaviour and loyalty variables. Among these variables, benefit is considered to provide the best segment for a marketer, since the main purpose for which products or services is bought by a customer is the benefits that they offer.

4.3.2 Industry Analysis

As indicated above market opportunity for a company depends not only on the size and nature of demand, but also on how well other companies are serving the demand. In assessing the extent and quality of service provided by competition, a useful starting point is to focus on an industry as a whole. The focus in this analysis is on the assessment of industry trends during the time period to be covered by the market opportunity analysis. Information required for this analysis includes:

- Industry growth in terms of output, sales, number of companies etc.
- Common operating practices which generally characterise the industry as a whole, including entry barriers, exit barriers, extent of credit facilities offered potential buyers etc.

Industry structure refers to the inter-relationship among different factors or forces that drive or characterise the behaviour of companies competing in that industry. Michael Porter's (1985) five forces model is one of the mainstream models for understanding the structure of industries and the forces that influence competitive behaviour. The model is based on the following considerations:

- The threat of new entrants into the industry
- The bargaining power of customers
- The bargaining power of suppliers
- The intensity of the rivalry among companies within the industry
- The potential for substitute products or services

The analysis of these five factors (forces) enables the manager to assess development trends within the industry and compare it with the strengths and weaknesses of his company. This offers him a basis for determining his strategy within the industry in general and within a specific market.

Threat of New Entrants

The degree of dynamism within an industry is indicated by the chances for new companies to be established. A company's ability to enter a new industry will depend upon what is referred to as *entry barriers*. Industries with high entry barriers tend to be rigidly structured and less dynamic and therefore raise the chances of good profit for the existing companies once there is a generally high level of business activity within the industry.

Entry barriers can result from capital requirement for starting the business, importance of economies of scale for operational costs, the degree of loyalty of existing customers towards specific brands, ability to find distributors for the products of a new entrant as well as specific government policies.

While entry barriers make it difficult for new companies to invest in the industry, *exit barriers* make it difficult for existing companies to divest once they have entered the business. For example substantial economies of scale in production are usually associated with specialised assets.

Where entry barriers are high and exit barriers are low new companies will be deterred from entering the industry and weaker competitors will leave the industry. In situations of high entry and exit barriers profit potentials will be high but this will be usually accompanied by more risk. The high exit barrier means that unsuccessful companies are compelled to stay on and adopt strategies that occasionally disturb the market, just to survive. In cases where entry barriers are low and exit barriers are low, many companies get started although their owners do not have the capacity to do serious business and enter merely for opportunistic reasons. They, however, become trapped during downturns in the market. If they are not able to leave, their existence results in overall excess capacity within the industry and thereby lead to low profitability.

Bargaining Power of Buyers

Customers of an industry's products can exert considerable pressure on companies within the industry to secure lower prices or better services. This is particularly possible under the following conditions:

- Buyers are very knowledgeable about industry's offerings and the technological basis of their production. This substantial knowledge will be advantageously used during bargaining situations. If the buyer is less knowledgeable skilled suppliers can convince them to pay higher prices for products that may not be different from those of their competitors.
- The volume and value of items bought by the customer is large. Buyers who purchase smaller volume/value of the company's product will have less incentive to pressure the company for a low price, since significant price reductions will have limited impact on the total purchase cost. Thus consumers of fresh pineapples in Europe may be less concerned about the unit price in the shops. But a distributor who makes large volume purchases from an exporter may press prices as

low as possible, if the purchases constitute a big proportion of the volume sold by the exporting company.

- The product is not considered as critical to the buyer. Buyers are more willing to pay premium prices for products that are considered to be of critical importance to them. Thus prices of drugs mean little to a sick person. Other products may not be assessed in the same way.
- Degree of concentration of buyers. When buyers are more concentrated than companies supplying the product are, they can often obtain better terms on prices and service. This is, for example, true with horticultural products such as tropical fruits and juices as well as coffee sold in European and North American markets. The available evidence shows a high concentration at the wholesaler/distributor point of the channel system, thereby making entry to these markets exceedingly difficult for smaller suppliers in Africa (Kuada and Sørensen, 2000).
- Product characteristics. Buyers also tend to be strong when they purchase standardised, undifferentiated products. This is because they can easily shift from one supplier to the other without this affecting the nature and quality of the products purchased. Commodities such as cocoa, coffee and steel satisfy these requirements. To some extent horticultural products such as fruits, vegetables and cut flowers are also relatively undifferentiated and give greater bargaining power to their importers/distributors.

Bargaining Power of Suppliers

Just as buyers can have stronger bargaining power than producers, suppliers of raw materials and inputs can also exhibit bargaining powers greater than producers under given circumstances. A producer that faces strong bargaining powers at both the supplier and the customer end of the value-chain tends to have a limited scope of strategic manoeuvre and must try to reduce his dependency. Developing country-based manufacturing companies can find themselves in such an uncomfortable situation, if they import their inputs from specific suppliers and sell small volume of standardised products to one or a few importers/distributors. Such a company is both dependent on the supplier and the distributor.

Suppliers can command substantial bargaining power over an industry under following conditions:

- The products are crucial to the buyer. Packaging materials are for example critical for the effective performance of logistics services for many companies. In countries where there are only a few suppliers of these materials, (as is frequently the case in a number of developing countries) most producers in the country become dependent on that company. Their ability to serve their customers effectively depends on the availability of the packaging materials supplied by the company. The latter naturally have a higher bargaining power over its customers.

- The products have high switching cost. Switching cost refers to the cost that the buying company will incur if it decides to switch from a given supplier's product to the use of products from another supplier. For example a switch from the use of one type of computer software to another may entail modifications in the entire information and administrative system of a unit in an organisation dependent on it. It may also entail elaborate training of staff and have implications for communication with the company's customers. In such a situation, companies using a particular type of software may feel reluctant to switch to another type of software in order to avoid the cost that it entails. In such a case the supplier of the software has a bargaining power over the buying companies.

- High concentration of suppliers. When suppliers are more concentrated than buyers are, they will tend to be in a better bargaining position over prices. Again, as long as there are few suppliers of packaging materials or the sale of these materials are done by a few distributors, they will have a high bargaining power. This is the underlying rationale for the establishment of OPEC and other commodity supplier organisations on the world market. Other industries may develop such a bargaining power through mergers and acquisitions that reduce fragmentation and raise their bargaining positions relative to buying companies.

- Suppliers' ability to enter the buying industry. Vertical integration is a strategy used by major suppliers to increase the added value of their products. Suppliers who make such intentions known to their major buyers may do so indirectly to pressurise them to accept higher prices for their products in an attempt to hold them back from investing directly in the industry.

4.3.3 Competitive intelligence and Competitor Analysis

Companies are eager to know if a new competitor is entering a foreign market, or has found a way to lower prices through more efficient production. It is also useful to know if a major competitor's new management team has streamlined a sloppy organization, leaving the company with reams of excess cash to spend on acquisitions. Having such information enables the company to redeploy its resources (money, time, manpower, and/or R&D efforts) to maximum effect.

Bradley (1995) argues that each company faces competition for its products and/or services from three sources. First, all products face generic competition. That is, each potential customer considers money spent on one item as an opportunity forgone for the expenditure on every other item. All buying opportunities are therefore seen as substitutes for each other. Second, competition can be experienced at product level. This is the kind of competition that attracts the attention of the market analyst. For example, tea and coffee may be in keen competition with each other but not with whisky. Third, products compete vigorously at brand level. That is, all tea producers selling in a particular market are in competition with each other. The nature and intensity of competition that a brand faces in a given market depends on the stage of evolution in the market. If the brand is the only one of its kind in the market, (i.e. at the pioneering stage of the market evolution), it naturally faces no competition at brand level but compete only with products that may be considered close substitutes to it. At a maturity stage, however, the product faces stiff competition.

Gaining insights into major competitors' goals will allow the analyst to determine whether or not the competitors are satisfied with their present positions in the market. It will also indicate whether they are likely to make new strategic moves in the near future or whether (and how aggressively) they will react to the entry of a new company into the market. The degree of threat competitors feel about the entry of another company will affect the probability of retaliation.

Companies engage in competitive intelligence to serve this purpose. Competitive intelligence is a field of strategic research that specializes in the collection and analysis of information about rival companies. It requires adherence to a strict ethical code by collecting bits of information that are available either in the public domain or from other players in the marketplace. The goal is to amass enough data to make meaningful comparisons between the company and its competitors — and to make better-informed strategic decisions as a result. The approach usually adopted is labelled *investigative research.*

4.3.4 Strategic Groups

Not all companies in an industry will present the same level of competition to the focal company. Some may have selected different target markets or may have substantially different marketing programmes that are not directly competing with the focal company. Porter (1985) introduces the concept of *strategic groups* to identify competitors whose marketing programmes must be closely investigated. As he explains it, a strategic group is the group of companies in an industry following the same or a similar strategy along a set of strategic dimensions such as quality and price. Usually there are a small number of strategic groups within an industry, each group pursuing a distinct set of strategy.

Companies in the same strategic group generally resemble each other closely in many ways, besides their broad strategies. Thus fresh pineapple exporters from African countries may constitute a strategic group in the international market, since their characteristics are very similar. They have all entered the market about the same time, are of relatively small sizes and earmark their products to the same target consumers.

A company's position within its strategic group will greatly impact its profitability in a given market. The company's position will in turn depend on the degree of competition within the strategic group, the scale of the company relative to others within the group, and the cost of entry into the group. It will also determine the ability of the company to execute its chosen strategy without invoking strong retaliation from other strategic group members.

In addition to the criteria mentioned above, it is imperative that the exporter determines whether his product has a *demonstrable competitive advantage* in the market segments of interest. The best measure of this is value-in-use analysis. Value-in-use is the worth of the producer's product when substituted for the product presently being used by customers within the particular market segment to satisfy his needs. If the value-in-use is greater than the price of the producer's product then his product has a demonstrable competitive advantage.

4.3.5 Channel Analysis

The marketing literature reminds us that getting the right channel partners is a key determinant of high market performance. Good channel partners play the following roles:

- They proactively search out for prospective customers.

- They have the skills and resources needed to close the business transactions
- They adopt win-win approach in addressing conflicts

In addition to that partners are key sources of information about customers and competitors that constitute the company's strategic group in the market.

Channel members are asked questions about product characteristics (including packaging product distinctiveness etc.) as well as the company's image in the eyes of the trade. The investigator also examines channel composition, market penetration of competing companies, advertising and pricing strategies.

Channel analysis helps the analyst to supplement the information he already has obtained through the other analyses and also gives him some indication as to the market entry strategies that the company should use. The following steps may help in the analysis:

1. List the number of relevant channel members in the market and draw a clear profile of each. The relevant channels are those who sell competitors' products (local and foreign) to the target markets that the company is interested in reaching. If the company expects to target the high end market, channel members serving those market segments must be considered and not those serving the low end markets. In drawing the profile of the channel members, the analyst must consider factors such as their size, distribution facilities, number of professional sales people and technical support personnel (if necessary), the geographical outreach of the sales, quality of products sold, image on the market and number of competitors served by the channel.

2. Assess the performance of channel members in the recent past. High growth channel members are more likely to have greater insight into trends in the target market and knowledge about customer preferences and expectation. This means they would be able to provide information about expected marketing strategy requirements in the focal market.

3. Select high profile channel members for interviews. The interview with channel members must aim at providing additional information to strengthen the segmentation analysis as well as size of demand in the different market segments. The interviewer should collect data from the channels on issues such as volume and value of sales during the immediate past as well as the various segments that buy from the company. If such data are not accessible, interviews could be of qualitative nature and highlight the expectations of the key sales persons with regard to changes in demand.

4.4 Market Performance Evaluation

Market selection is just the beginning of international market activities. Having entered the selected market, companies must make sure that their marketing objectives are achieved through timely delivery of required goods and services and the overall satisfaction of their customers. To determine the extent to which the company's marketing activities are contributing to the attainment of the desired objectives, the company must monitor its market performance in a variety of ways. The three most popular types of analysis conducted for this purpose are (1) market gap analysis, (2) customer value analysis, and (3) share of purchase analysis. They are described briefly below.

4.4.1 Market Gap Analysis

Going back to the military analogy, companies are advised to cover all bases as part of their marketing strategy. This strategy, also called product proliferation, entails introducing new products to ensure a full product line or to fill gaps in the market. Covering all bases may involve introducing multiple versions of a product in terms of models or product types. Many companies carry full product lines to block access to the industry by new entrants.

The primary aim of Market Gap Analysis is to assess the performance of one's company's products within the market and determine marketing functions that require adjustment in order to achieve optimum results. Two main stages are involved in the analytical process:

1. Estimating the total sales potential attainable for each product line, and
2. Performing gap analysis to explain why a company's sales fall short of the market forecast for the product lines.

Information about the sales and profits of each item in the product lines and how the product lines compare with competitors' product lines is very useful for strategic marketing decisions. The Gap Analysis simply assumes that the difference between a company's actual sales of a given product line and the total sales of that product can be accounted for by one or a combination of four conditions. These are:

1. Incomplete product line served on the market.
2. Incomplete coverage of the market due to poor distribution.
3. Limited usage of the product within the market segments served.
4. The strength of the competitive forces on the market.

This implies that the Gap Analysis involves four partial analyses:

1. Analysis of product line gap
2. Analysis of distribution gap
3. Analysis of usage gap
4. Analysis of competitive gap.

These analyses together describe the focal company's market structure profile. The aim of these analyses is to determine their relative importance in explaining the gap between the potential and the actual sales.

The order in which the analysis is undertaken is very important. For example, since it makes little sense to recognise a distribution gap for product lines that are not included in the company's product portfolio, a product gap analysis must precede an analysis of distribution gaps for the various products. Similarly, usage gap analysis becomes important after the product line gaps and distribution gaps have been ascertained. The reason is that incomplete product line and inadequate distribution are eventually reflected in limited usage. By improving the first two, the sales that can be generated through closing usage gap increases.

Coming to competitive gap analysis, it must be noted that some of competitors' strengths in a particular market may be due to the wider range of product lines they offer or the coverage and effectiveness of their distribution networks in covering the market segments. Thus by performing product gap analysis and distribution gap analysis, part of the competitive gap analysis is being performed. In conducting competitive gap analysis, therefore, one concentrates on dimensions other than product portfolio and distribution strengths that seem to account for the better performance of competitors relative to your company.

Product Gap Analysis

The main steps in the product gap analysis are as follows:

1. List all the alternative elements with which the products that serve the same need can be identified - e.g. size, options, style, colour, flavour, form and quality.
2. Estimate the relative share of each of the variables (sizes, styles, colour etc.) of the total sales for the market.

Assume, for example, that the product line on the market is identified by three elements each accounting for 33.3% of the total sales. If your company sells products with only 2 of the elements, it then has 33.3% product line gap. In other words, it has 33.3% market potential to capture by closing the product line gap. Let us take a concrete example. Pineapple can be sold as fresh, sliced and canned or as juice. If the three elements in the product line represent 33.3% of the market each and the company in question sells only fresh pineapples, we can safely conclude that it has a product line gap of 66.6%.

A company that is trying to cover all bases may face one or more of the following difficulties. First, some companies, especially the small ones, may not have the resources to offer a full product line. Second, product proliferation may cause a company to spread its resources too thinly, violating the principle of concentration of forces at the decisive point. Covering too many markets and over extending itself, leaves a company vulnerable to competitor attacks, as it makes for an easy target. Third, this strategy cannot fully protect a company from attacks by other competitors who wish to enter the industry. Even if a company was able to cover the major segments, it is impossible to cover every possible niche in the market. This allows small companies to enter the market and occupy these niches. These niches, although small and unattractive at the time, often explode into large segments posing a threat to established companies.

Distribution Gap Analysis

The steps in the distribution gap analysis are as follows:

1. List all the alternative distribution channels that carry the product line in question as well as their corresponding geographical coverage.

2. Determine their relative proportion of the total sales at a given point in time.
3. Determine which of these outlets do not carry your company's product and why.
4. Determine the volume of potential sales you lose by not achieving the required market penetration through these outlets.
5. Assess the required investment to achieve this coverage relative to the pay-off in terms of increased sales/margin.

Following up on our pineapple example, fresh pineapples can be sold through chain supermarkets with wider range of outlets or through smaller grocery stores with limited geographical coverage. Let us assume that chain supermarkets account for 80% of all pineapple sales in the company's chosen market but its importers sell to only smaller grocery stores. This means the company's pineapples do not reach a larger segment of the potential market, i.e. those who shop only in chain supermarkets.

Several reasons account for differences in the size of distribution gap that a company may face in various countries. One possible reason is that the company may not be able to sell the category of products that the distribution channels are interested in. Another reason may be that distributors may not find the company attractive do deal with if the company is unable to fulfil the distributors' purchasing conditions. For example, some major chain-stores may require their suppliers to be able to fulfil a minimum volume of orders at specific intervals before they are considered attractive. Suppliers that are unable to fulfil these conditions may be deemed unattractive.

By analysing these conditions management should determine the economic feasibility of closing the distribution gap in the focal market and adopt the appropriate strategies.

Usage Gap Analysis

The size of usage gaps may also differ from one country to the other. Differences may be due to variations in the proportions of potential users who do not use the relevant product, i.e. the "non-user" component of the target market. They can also be due to differences in the size of usage, i.e. the proportion of heavy users in the market segment or even the frequency of usage. For example, European families use fresh pineapples on specific occasions or as an ingredient in the preparation of desert. Families with younger children are likely to use it more frequently than single member households. All these consumer characteristics would produce variations in the usage gaps in different countries. Again, the results of the analysis provide pointers to the strategic choices that the company must consider.

Competitive Gap Analysis

Companies face different competitive situations in different market environments. There may be variations in the profile (i.e. strengths and weaknesses) of local as well as foreign competitors operating in each country. The focus of this aspect of the gap analysis is on companies that constitute the strategic group of the company. By noting the strengths of the other companies in the group, relative to the focal company, the analyst can guide managers in choosing a combination of strategies that would sustain the company's competitive position within the group.

4.4.2 Customer Value Analysis

Customer Value Analysis (CVA) is based on the concept of customer-oriented marketing introduced in chapter 1. Basically, customers choose between suppliers by evaluating which supplier provides them with the best *value*. The CVA may start with internal sources of data, drawing on existing information that the vendor already possesses about each customer- sales volume, profits generated, growth trends, technical strengths etc. The analyst may also conduct sample surveys of the client company's customers and of its competitors' customers to determine the relative performance of the company on many attributes ranging from product quality and technology to pricing and sales support. The CVA proceeds along the following steps:

1. Create a profit profile comparing the profit contribution of each customer.
2. Determine the source of the profit.
3. Assess the value elements beyond profits – i.e. the relational value of each customer
4. Determine the overall value ranking within the customer group.
5. Determine the marketing requirements for serving the customers.
6. Develop a sales/marketing programme commensurate with the

customer's value

The first three steps allow the vendor to assess the total value of each of the customers. An assessment of the profit contributions of existing customers involves determining sales and profits by each principal product line supplied to the customer. The profit analysis requires detailed breakdown of marketing costs assignable to the products sold to the customer, including order processing costs and field service costs. Customers are then ranked in terms of profitability. Overall profit obtained from a customer may come from many different sources. It may be due to the frequency of orders, sizes of orders, share of customers' total purchases and location of the customer. All these profit determinants require close attention. These analyses may be done in three steps:

1. Assessment of the growth (or decline) that is expected to occur in each customer's demand for the vendor's products.
2. Assessment of the degree of market risk associated with each customer.
3. Assessment of the marketing efforts required to satisfy the needs of the current buyer mix.

Figure 4.2 provides an illustration of the dimensions and considerations that go into customer value analysis. The main dimensions in this analysis are the market-perceived quality profile and the market-perceived price profile. These dimensions provide an indication of how much worse or better the client company is doing within the target market.

Figure 4.2: A Framework for Customer Value Analysis

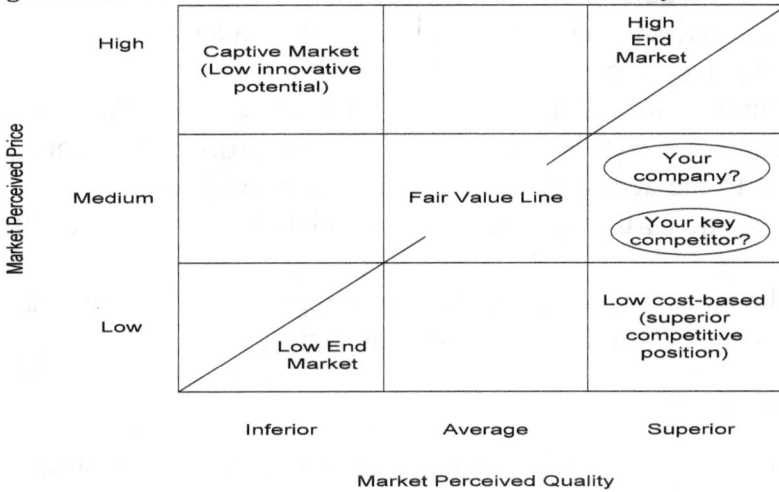

Source: Kuada (2008)

4.4.3 Share of Purchase Analysis

The vendor is particularly interested in noticing significant changes in customers' demand for the vendor's products. This is done by undertaking "share of purchase" (share of wallet) analysis which provides an indication of changes in the customers' purchases. Distinction is usually drawn between present and future sales gap. The present sales gap is the difference between actual sales to the customer of a given product/service and customers' total purchase volume of product/service. Thus, if the vendor supplies only 30% of the total purchases made by the customer of the product in question, the sales gap is 70%. The future sales gap is based on the customer's projected demand of the product/service in question. A customer that has a superior competitive position within a growing market is likely to increase its demand for inputs at least in proportion to the market growth rate.

Apart from an assessment of the customer's contribution to the business marketer's total sales, it is also important to evaluate it in terms of (a) capacity to develop the vendor's image (b) contribution to vendor's know-how development, and (c) new market development potential, the so called network effect. For example, a small electronic company in Northern Jutland may pride itself in supplying unique components to a major international company such as Nokia, Ericsson or IBM. This would enhance the company's standing within the industry as a serious and reliable supplier. A vendor may also keep within its buyer mix, customers that do not contribute substantially to its sales but provide challenging and innovative ideas that are of strategic importance to its overall competitive profile. The network effect refers to the access that a customer can provide to new markets or market segments through networks of relationships with potential customers.

A vendor must prune its customer mix regularly to ensure that its customer profile can fulfil its marketing objectives.

4.5 Summary

This chapter presents an integrated framework for the analysis of market opportunities available to a given firm in a given country. The framework suggests that management is usually interested in knowing three things:

1. The size of a particular market and its growth rate.
2. The marketing requirements to serve the customers in that market.
3. Competitors' marketing strategies in that market and customers perception of the effectiveness of these strategies.

In other words, the outcome of each market analysis should address these three issues. The information required would be obtained by undertaking the following five analyses:

1. Demand analysis
2. Segmentation analysis
3. Industry analysis
4. Competitor analysis
5. Channel analysis

The marketing and strategic management literature provides variety of guidelines for undertaking these analyses and the reader is advised to refer to these sources for additional guidelines and inspiration to be able to undertake his analysis.

References

Bradley, Frank (1995) *International Marketing Management* 5th Edition (Harlow, Prentice Hall)

Kotler, P., (1994) *Marketing Management: Analysis, Planning, Implementation, and Control*: 8th Edition (New York, Prentice Hall)

Kuada, J., (2008) *International Market Analysis – Theories and Methods* (London, Adonis and Abbey)

Kuada, J. and O. J. Sørensen (2000) *Internationalization of Companies from Developing Countries,* (New York, NY: Haworth Press)

Porter, Michael E. (1985), *Competitive Advantage – Creating and Sustaining Superior Performance.* (New York: The Free Press)

Toyne, Brian and Walters, Peter G.P., (1989) *Global Marketing Management: A Strategic Perspective* (Mass. Allyn and Bacon)

For Further Readings

Albaum, G, Duerr, E., and Strandskov, J., (2005) *International Marketing and Export Management* - 5th Edition (Pearson Education Ltd., England)

Douglas, Susan P., and Craig, C. S., (1983) *International Marketing Research* (New Jersey, Prentice-Hall International)

CHAPTER FIVE

Market-Driving Strategies

5.1 Introduction

Conventional management thinking encourages companies to focus on matching and beating their rivals. They are to do so by adopting market-driven strategies. These strategies frequently result in head-to-head competition based largely on incremental improvements in cost, quality, or both within the prevailing market space. As the market space gets crowded, prospects for profits and growth are reduced, and cut-throat competition drains the energy of individuals and their entire organisations.

Few scholars have recommended an alternative approach. They advise companies (small and large) to develop a culture that allows their employees to act individually and jointly to think outside the box, challenging deeply held assumptions, and combining different, often seemingly unrelated kinds of expertise and knowledge (Watts, 2004). They argue that this will result in creating new market spaces and opportunities that will make competition irrelevant and enable companies to create new value propositions together with their customers and explore hitherto unknown business opportunities. The concepts of value innovation, creative intelligence and market driving strategies derive from this perspective. This chapter provides an overview of the reasons and methods that guide a market driving approach to business strategies.

5.2 Creativity and Market Driving Strategies

"Take the road less taken, as it will lead you to new discoveries", goes a popular saying. Pablo Picasso was quoted as saying, "I am always doing things I can't do, that's how I get to do them". In a similar vein, the jazz pianist Keith Jarrett has been quoted as saying "I think the fear of failure is why I try things ... if I see that there is some value in something and I'm not sure whether I deserve to attempt it, I want to find out.". These statements carry useful messages for high achieving business managers who seek to sustain the competitive advantages of their companies. It strikes at the core of creativity and underscores the ability of individuals and groups to create values and find new solutions to existing problems.

Creativity is generally understood in the business literature simply as an ability to take risks, and ask new questions which could generate novel, original and valuable ideas. In that sense all humans with normal capacities are able to exhibit at least moderate levels of creativity in their work life. It is also believed that the social environment can influence both the level and the frequency of creative behaviour. Companies that make creativity the cornerstone of their business models tend to facilitate the development of products, and processes that enhance their performance (Sadi and Al-Dubaisi, 2008). People, processes, organizational structures and the right cultural orientation must be in place for creativity to occur in organizations (Amabile, 1996). Organizations that have those conditions tend to motivate individual employees to go beyond the call of duty and exert energy and initiative to the best of their abilities and assume ownership of the value innovation processes in their organizations. Some scholars argue that the creative potentials of organizations tend to be magnified when employees work in concert and approach creativity in a systematic manner (Amabile, 1996; Amabile *et al.*, 2004). Managers are therefore encouraged to build teams of employees with divergent knowledge bases and provide them with internal working conditions that can enhance their joint creative efforts. As Hargadon and Bechky (2006) observe, creative teams look at organizational problems in different ways, making unexpected links among apparently discrepant elements of information, developing new solutions to problems as and when they appear rather than mastering and constantly reapplying standard methods.

Barrett (1998) explains the jazz pianist Keith Jarrett's observations about jazz music by arguing that jazz players constitute a group of diverse specialists living in a chaotic, turbulent environment; making fast, irreversible decisions; highly interdependent on one another to interpret equivocal information; dedicated to innovation and the creation of novelty. But jazz bands improvise coherently and maximise social innovation in a coordinated fashion. This is why they nearly succeed each time, producing something new, charting new territories and creating new values. Thus, creativity is best seen as multi-dimensional and group endeavours rather than discoveries made by talented individuals in isolation.The jazz analogy may be seen as a living symbol of value innovation. Just 50 years ago many multi-billion dollar industries of today did not exist. Google, Yahoo, Microsoft, Bodyshop, Starbucks were not established. In simple terms, they came into existence as manifestations of the innovative capabilities of groups of individuals. This is what market-driving strategies are about. They are strategies that embrace innovative changes in the logic of industry and business systems.

It is also important to note that market driving strategies are predicated on the awareness that customers may not always provide useful information for business strategy formulations. This is because when asked about their wants, customers lack imagination to suggest radical changes in products. Furthermore, consumers act highly rationally within some set of false beliefs resulting in buying predictions that may not be validated by subsequent actions. Thus, businesses cannot fully understand the needs of their customers by asking them, since most customers may not have imaginations stretching beyond their immediate circumstances. By thinking with customers and reaching beyond their immediate requirements, businesses are engaged in creating new markets for themselves by offering values that enable their customers to create new markets themselves. This is what the concept of co-creation is about.

There are different levels of market-driving strategy based on value proposition and value chain. Managers must particularly design strategies aimed at the following (potential) consumer segments: (a) underserved market (b) un-served markets, and (c) incipient market segments – i.e. reaching beyond existing demand and unlocking a new mass of customers that did not exist before. Without a market-driving strategy, a marketing plan focusing solely on the *served* market is incomplete as it risks losing the underserved or *un-served* markets (sometimes even bigger than current customers) to other competitors.

97

Thus, market-driving strategy should be viewed as a source of innovation and growth for old businesses.

5.3 Blue Ocean Strategy

In 2005 W. Chan Kim and Renée Mauborgne from INSEAD published the book Blue Ocean Strategy - How to Create Uncontested Market Space and Make Competition Irrelevant. It quickly became a best seller because it provided a new strategic direction to many managers. They also popularised the concept of value innovation in that publication.

Kim and Mauborgne based their views on years of investigations of the strategic orientation of different companies in different industries. Their study showed that the strategic thinking of less successful companies was dominated by the idea of staying ahead of the competition. Typically, to grow their share of a market, companies strive to retain and expand existing customers. This often leads to finer segmentation and greater tailoring of offerings to better meet customer preferences. The more intense the competition is the greater, on average, is the resulting customization of offerings. As companies compete to embrace customer preferences through finer segmentation, they often risk creating too-small target markets. In stark contrast, the high-growth companies paid little attention to matching or beating their rivals. Instead, they sought to make their competitors irrelevant through a strategic logic that they called value innovation. That is, value innovative companies break free from the pack by staking out fundamentally new market space by creating products or services for which there are no direct competitors. For example, when the founders of Facebook created the site, they were engaged in blue ocean strategy simply because it was a new site that served a purpose no other site did.

They then developed the terms red and blue oceans to provide a symbolic picture of the contrasts in the strategic orientations of the consistently successful and less successful companies. Red oceans are all the industries in existence today - the known market space. In red oceans, industry boundaries are defined and accepted, and the competitive rules of the game are known. Blue oceans, in contrast, represent all the industries not in existence today. In blue oceans, demand is created rather than fought over, and there is ample opportunity for growth.

They argued that the creation of blue oceans is a product of strategy and managerial action, not of the size or age of the company or the conditions they are up against. Managers must be consistently engaged in strategic moves that create new blue oceans since competitors are always ready to crowd into new markets by imitating best practices of the value innovators. But many managers are not sure how to create blue oceans.

Blue ocean strategy is therefore about challenging assumptions about strategy, redefining market boundaries and making the competition irrelevant rather than competing on established ground. It is geared towards creating new market space and encompasses the entire value chain from product, service and delivery, and costs to pricing, instead of any one function. This perspective is therefore consistent with Argyris and Schön's (1978) single and double (or meta-) loop learning.

Blue ocean strategy therefore requires a different competitive mind-set and a systematic way of looking for opportunities. Instead of searching within the conventional boundaries of industry competition, managers can look methodically across those boundaries to find unoccupied territory that represents real value innovation.

Kim and Mauborgne offer the following guidelines to companies in the blue ocean strategy formulation process:

1. Do not compete in existing market space instead you should create uncontested market space.
2. Do not beat the competition instead you should make the competition irrelevant.
3. Do not exploit existing demand instead you should create and capture new demand.
4. Do not make the value/cost trade-off instead you should break the value/cost trade-off.
5. Do not align the whole system of a company's activities with its strategic choice of differentiation or low cost instead you should align the whole system of a company's activities in pursuit of both differentiation and low cost.

Making new product/service offering involves more than simply "getting close to the customer". It entails being a step ahead of customers and completely understanding the market in order to be able to reconstruct the customer value attributes. Marketing scholars have observed that customers may not always provide useful information for business strategy formulations (Dickinson et al. 1986; Day, 1990). This is because when asked about their wants, customers lack imagination to suggest radical changes in products. Furthermore, consumers act highly rationally within some set of false beliefs resulting in buying predictions that may not be validated by subsequent actions. Thus businesses cannot fully understand the needs of their customers by asking them, since most customers may not have imaginations stretching beyond their immediate circumstances. By thinking with customers and reaching beyond their immediate requirements, businesses are engaged in creating new markets for themselves by offering values that enable their customers to create new markets themselves.

To do so businesses must ask four fundamental questions:

- Which of the attributes that the industry takes for granted should be eliminated?
- Which of these attributes should be reduced well below the industry standard?
- Which of these attributes should be raised above industry standards?
- Which of these attributes should be created that the industry has never offered?

The process of analysis that enables the company to answer these questions helps the company to distinguish between the "nice to haves" and the "need to haves" of the product/service package that companies must offer their customers. It also helps in identifying areas of cost reduction. In the process the company identifies which costs should be raised and which ones should be reduced with the net effect that overall cost tends to be reduced while the value offered to the segment of the market targeted is raised. This is how the traditional value-cost tradeoff tends to be broken. Thus instead of following the conventional logic of outpacing the competition by offering a better solution to the given problem, the company offers a better solution to a new problem and thereby raises the overall value of the offering to the customer. This is the logic guiding the concept of value innovation. Said differently, value innovation is not an "add-on"; it is a new business platform.

Kim and Maubrogne argue further that successful value innovation needs to have a compelling "value proposition" for buyers, a "profit proposition" for companies and a "people proposition" for employees and partners to ensure that they execute blue-ocean ideas with speed and precision. It is this whole-system approach, integrating a company's functional and operational activities, that makes the creation of blue oceans a sustainable strategy. Thus, blue ocean strategy may be considered as a subset of market-driving strategies. Whereas market-driven strategies go for customer retention and loyalty, market-driving strategies pursue customer acquisition. Whereas the former's performance is gauged on market shares gained, the latter's performance is gauged on market penetration and acceptance.

Kim and Mauborgne's work has been very much criticised as nothing more than an excellent marketing endeavour, based on the originality and intrigue of its title and subtitle as well as the introduction of captivating new labels. But, on the whole, it is a combination of several old concepts and views expressed by many other authors (Gandellini, and Venanzi, 2011). But it certainly provides new perspectives of the previously well-known concepts. Furthermore, it offers a comprehensive systematization of the strategic process that allows the identification and exploitation of new industry sectors and market spaces and therefore provides theoretical and empirical grounding for market driving strategies.

5. 4 Purple Ocean Strategies

Barwise and Meehan (2012) argue that, while conceptually useful, there is no clear cut distinction between red ocean and blue ocean environments in the real business world and that it is impossible to make competition irrelevant for a long time period. They therefore argue for a new label - purple oceans. Purple ocean strategies are supposed to combine some of the characteristics of the red-ocean and blue ocean strategies. What happens in practice is that competitors quickly discover the new business opportunity presented by a blue ocean company and quickly erode the first mover-advantages created. The company therefore needs to engage in incremental innovative practices in order to extend the duration of these advantages.

Winning strategies in purple oceans include unique positioning and low cost combined with clear communication ("customer promise"), trust (through reliable delivery and prompt handling of customer complaints), and guaranteeing customer satisfaction (through continually improving the promises). In addition to these, companies must continuously "innovate beyond the familiar", and adapt rapidly to changing customer expectations. Companies must also focus on clear brand promises and improve the brand promise on a continuous basis.

Thus, successful and sustainable performance requires the adoption of some aspects of blue and red ocean strategies – the appropriate blend being based on company history, resources and values. At any given point in time some products and services may find themselves in transitional stages, moving in-between the cells. For example, companies may find some of their services being considered as stars by some segments of the market while other segments may consider them question marks. The main strategic challenge for companies is how to manage these interfaces between the cells when the services cannot neatly fit into any category. Thus, to stay relevant to customers on a sustained basis, companies must continue to look across alternative industries and across strategic groups within industries in order to identify new opportunities and focus their creative resources in order to take advantage of these opportunities.

I have suggested above that the establishment of Facebook was a clear example of blue ocean strategy. But aspects of Facebook's strategies are not entirely blue ocean-oriented. The company has in some regards been battling with competitors by creating features that it claims are "unrelated" to other networks, despite the fact that those features serve a need other platforms already supplied. Facebook, today, is therefore engaged more in purple ocean strategies than blue-ocean strategies. The message here is that a company must not strive to create an uncontested market space if it does not have the capabilities to do so. It can improve its performance and sustain its competitive advantages by adopting purple ocean strategies and minimizing its need to engage in defensive attacks with its major competitors. A smart strategy is one of cost-effective incremental innovations – i.e. giving customers a feeling of "newness" in a company's existing services, a value that they will be willing to pay for.

5.5   Radical innovation and Market Driving Strategies

Another concept that underscores the importance of market driving strategies in highly competitive business environments is radical innovation. John Rockefeller is quoted as saying "if you want to succeed, you have to forge new paths and avoid borrowed ones." This is true with companies that adopt market driving approach to their businesses. It is fascinating and self-actualizing when a CEO is able to provide a leadership that produces game changing innovations within its industry, shocking rivals and leaving them to look on from the side-lines. In common language, radical innovation implies "doing what the company did not do before" – i.e. a discontinuity with the past. Radical innovations create dramatic change in processes, products, or services and thereby transform existing markets or industries, or create new ones. Thus, these types of innovations are also referred to as *disruptive innovations.* High level of uncertainty is their hallmark; they are significantly risky, take more time to develop and can be expensive. It is often said that successful radical innovations occur infrequently within any particular area (perhaps once every 5 – 10 years).

It is important to bear in mind that companies engaged in radical innovations do not necessarily have to invent new technologies. They may find new combinations of existing technologies and produce solutions that others have not earlier considered. For example, one of the radical innovations frequently cited in the innovation literature is Apple's development of multi-touch interfaces and their associated gestures to control handheld and desktop systems. Apple did not invent either the multi-touch interfaces or gestural control. Multi-touch systems have been in computer and design laboratories for over 20 years prior to their application by Apple. The gestures also have a long history. Although Apple's ideas were not radical to the scientific community, they did come as a radical, major shift in the world of products and how people interact with them and give meaning to them.

Most radical innovations take considerable time to become accepted because they seldom live up to their potential when first introduced. Diffusion of Innovation (DOI) theory helps explain how, why, and at what rate such innovations are adopted and spread through cultures, operating at the individual and company level. It sees innovations as being communicated through certain channels over time and within a particular social system. Individuals are seen as possessing different degrees of willingness to adopt innovations, and thus it is generally observed that the portion of the population adopting an innovation is approximately normally distributed over time. Breaking this normal distribution into segments leads to the classification of people into the following five categories (from earliest to latest adopters): innovators, early adopters, early majority, late majority, laggards (Rogers, 1995). The innovation process in organizations is much more complex. It generally involves a number of individuals, perhaps including both supporters and opponents of the new idea, each of whom plays a role in the innovation-decision.

The task of marketing managers is to ensure that potential adopters are well-informed about the existence of the innovation and can evaluate the opportunity of adopting by comparing gross benefits (drivers) and costs (obstacles) from acquiring and using the products. The prevailing understanding in the literature is that the process by which customers adopt radical innovations is influenced by the characteristics of the innovation as perceived by the potential adopters, customers' needs and expectations, and, features of the competitive environment. In b2b situations factors such as size of the potential customer organization, age, and capabilities are also considered among the key determinants. The competitive environment can be described by the degree of company concentration, the level of prices, and the existence of informational spillovers among potential users. Attributes of the innovation are usually related to technical features (i.e. compatibility with existing solutions) and may vary depending on the perception of potential adopters.

It has also been argued that even if potential adopters expect an innovation to be useful, they may find it too difficult to use, so that the performance benefits may be perceived to be low when compared with the costs of learning. Thus, the extent to which an innovation is perceived as relatively difficult to understand and use - its *complexity* or *perceived difficulty of use* - is also an important variable. The knowledge required to use a radical innovation successfully may place a great demand on potential users. Users differ in their knowledge and skills with respect to a specific innovation and may perceive different levels of complexity in its use. If some individuals cannot use the innovation because it requires a different knowledge base from the one they possess, they are likely to experience a process of 'social exclusion' (Rogers, 1995).

A useful marketing strategy aimed at overcoming some of these adoption barriers is to provide potential adopters the opportunity to see the usage of the innovation demonstrated in real life – a strategy usually referred to as *trialability*. Rip (1995) argues that functioning, real world examples are often more important than arguments about advantages and expected functions.

5.6 Summary

Successful marketing strategies entail being a step ahead of your customers and completely understanding the market in order to be able to reconstruct the customer value attributes. It is now generally acknowledged in academic and practitioner business literature that adopting a market driving strategy the company will concentrate its efforts and resources in satisfying needs not yet satisfied. This is likely to result in better profits for the company (instead of cutthroat competition) and better opportunities for employees to grow. Thus, there are internal marketing advantages in adopting a market driving strategy.

Thus, this perspective shifts the search for competitive advantages of organizations from such other resources as tangible assets and finance, to intangible and metaphysical process. The understanding is that the ability of organizations to facilitate the flow of positive energy is critical to its long term survival and growth. For business companies, this is the most important source of sustainable competitive advantage. Employees in organizations with positive energy flows would see their work as fulfilling a higher purpose and would be willing to do their very best in spite of challenging work conditions. They would focus on solutions rather than complain about problems.

Research shows that companies that dominate one generation of technology often fail to maintain leadership in the next because these industry leaders continue investing in incremental improvements in the technologies that made them successful even when more effective disruptive technologies appear on the horizon.

Marketing radically innovative products/services may entail social and cultural mobilization that may excite the targeted consumers.

In effect, companies can sustain their competitive positions for many decades into the future if they change the mindset of the management and employees from being less customer-oriented to being more customer-focused. This implies that the strategic orientation of the companies must be both proactive and reactive. The reactive strategies respond to explicitly articulated customer needs, while the proactive strategies seek to explore hitherto unknown business opportunities through value innovation.

References

Amabile, T.M. (1996), *Creativity in Context*, (Boulder, Westview Press)

Amabile, T.M., Schatzel, E.A., Moneta, G.B., and Kramer, S.J. (2004), "Leader behaviours and the work environment for creativity: perceived leader support", *Leadership Quarterly* 15 pp. 5–32

Barrett, Frank, J., (1998) "Creativity and Improvisation in Jazz and Organizations: Implications" *Organization Science* Vol 9, No.5. pp: 605–22

Barwise, P., & Meehan, S. (2012) "Innovation beyond blue oceans" *Market Leader*, (Q4), 24–27.

Day, G.S. (1990) *Marketing Driven Strategy Process for Creating Value* (New York, Free Press)

Gandellini, G., &Venanzi, D. (2011) "Purple Ocean Strategy: How to Support SMEs' Recovery"*Procedia-Social and behaviour al Sciences*, 24, 1-15

Hargadon, A. B., &Bechky, B. A. (2006) "When collections of creatives become creative collectives: A field study of problem solving at work"*Organization Science*, Vol. 17 No.4 pp: 484-500.

Kim, W. Chan and Mauborgne, Renée (2005) *Blue Ocean Strategy How to Create Uncontested Market Space and make the Competition Irrelevant* (Boston: Harvard Business School Press)

Rogers, E. M. (1995) *Diffusion of innovations* - 4th Ed (New York: Free Press)

Rip, A. (1995) "Introduction of new technology: Making use of recent insights from sociology and economics of technology"*Technology Analysis & Strategic Management*, 7, 417-431.

Sadi, Muhammad Asad and Al-Dubaisi, Ali H., (2008) "Barriers to organizational creativity: The marketing executives' perspective in Saudi Arabia" *Journal of Management Development* Vol. 27 Iss. 6 pp: 574 - 599

Watts, Duncan (2004) "Decentralized Intelligence"Originally posted on the Slate website on Aug. 5, 2004 Available at: http://www.leader-values.com/Content/detail.asp?ContentDetailID=952

For Further Readings

Carrillat, F., Jaramillo, F. and Locander, W. (2004), "Market-Driving Organisations: A Framework", *Academy of Marketing Science Review*, No. 5, pp. 1-14.

Kumar N., Scheer, L., and Kotler, P. (2000), "From Market Driven to Market Driving", *European Management Journal*, Vol. 18 (February), pp. 129-42

Hills, S. and Sarin, S. (2003), "From market driven to market driving: an alternate paradigm for marketing in high technology industries", *Journal of Marketing Theory and Practice*, Vol. 11 No. 3, pp. 13-24.

Harris, L. and Cai, K. (2002), "Exploring Market Driving: A Case Study of De Beers in China", *Journal of Market-Focused Management* (May), pp. 171-96.

CHAPTER SIX

Internal Marketing and Market-Oriented Strategies

6.1 Introduction

I have argued in chapter five that although it is laudable to pursue market-driving strategies, very few firms do so with success. Companies need to exploit the gains of their innovations and, since they cannot keep competition entirely away for many years,it is advisable for them to pursue a purple ocean strategy.This allows them to strike a healthy balance between the huge risks associated with going out all alone in an uncertain business environment and gains of such initiatives. This will also set them on a stronger, profitable, and sustained growth trajectory in a competitive business environment. Purple ocean strategies require companies to be market-oriented – i.e. adopt market-driven strategies.

It has also been noted that whether or not a customer perceives a company as delivering the products and services promised in a consistent manner depends on the attitudes, commitment and behaviour of their employees. The management literature shows that work attitude is partly shaped by organizational culture. As Narver and Slater (1990) explain it, customer-orientation is nothing less than an organisational culture which enlists the participation of all employees for purposes of creating superior value for a company's customers and superior performance for itself. The marketing literature has therefore developed the concept of "internal marketing" to explain the manner in which the internal relationship between an organization and its employees impacts its value delivery capabilities. The aim of this chapter is to provide an overview of the main arguments supporting market orientation (market-driven strategies) and internal marketing strategies.

6.2 Characteristics of a Market- driven Company

As indicated in the introduction to this chapter, market-oriented companies are those that are highly sensitive to the needs of their customers and proactively take steps to fulfil these needs. Some of the needs may be well articulated by current or potential customers. But there are also occasions where customers are not readily aware of what is technologically possible or how technologies that are soon to be available can fulfil their needs. This means market-oriented companies must be a step ahead of their customers and suggest new services to them even before they become available on the market. It is this proactive orientation that provides a market-oriented company a sustainable competitive advantage in an increasingly dynamic business environment. It enables such companies to satisfy their customers better, faster and/or more cheaply than their competitors.

Market-oriented companies have other defining characteristics. First, they are capable of responding quickly to competitor challenges and are able to spot any evidence of customer dissatisfaction. Second, they are also able to quickly detect changes in customer needs and product preferences and take the necessary actions in response to the information. Third, they are also effective in getting all business functions to work together to provide superior customer value. Thus, Narver and Slater (1990) perceive market-oriented companies as those that are:

- *Customer-oriented,* i.e. gaining intimate insight into customers' needs and market service requirements;
- *Competitor-oriented*, i.e., gaining understanding of competitors' capabilities and market response patterns; and
- Exhibit *inter-functional co-ordination*, i.e., coordinating the utilization of company resources to create superior customer value.

The importance of market information generation as a characteristic of market-oriented businesses has been emphasised by other scholars. For example, Kohli and Jaworski (1990) define market orientation as being composed of three business characteristics:

- Company-wide generation of market intelligence, pertaining to current and future customer needs.
- Dissemination of this intelligence among departments of the company.
- Company-wide response to the knowledge derived from the market intelligence.

In other words, market-oriented companies are expected to gather, interpret and use market information in a more systematic, thoughtful and anticipatory manner than less market-oriented companies.

Building on what we know about high-performing market-oriented businesses, a company can describe itself as truly customer-oriented if it brings the voices of its customers to the centre stage of key decisions. In more practical terms, it means that such a company must take deliberate steps to increase its knowledge of its customers. This may be done by requiring all employees that interact with customers to listen attentively to the customers and register the information they provide systematically and share such information with other employees. It also means gathering information systematically from other sources than customers and analysing the information available in the company's database – a process frequently referred to as *data mining.*

Managers in a market-driven company assume that customers have full knowledge of their needs and are willing to reveal these needs when asked about them. The strategy of companies managed with such an assumption can be described mainly as reactive – i.e. reacting effectively to declared customer needs. To do so, the company must possess distinctive capabilities and resource configuration which allows it be agile – i.e. adapt swiftly to changing customer needs (Day, 1994).

It is important to note that there is a difference between building a market-driven (or customer-oriented) business culture and a *customer-compelled* business culture. The marketing literature describes customer-compelled companies as those which bend over backwards to whatever customers want, trying to be everything for every single customer. In their zeal to be customer-oriented, they are unable to focus and discipline their marketing strategies. Marketing costs increase more than the customer values they deliver, leading to low profitability. This is bad management. It may lead to the collapse of the company thereby making its customers, employees, shareholders and the company itself losers.

6.3 Incremental Innovation and Market Driving Strategies

We have earlier noted that companies that adopt market driving strategies normally stimulate creative efforts that produce radical innovations. Similarly, market-driven strategies encourage incremental innovation that enhances usage features and experiences to users of their products allowing them to enjoy better performance or reductions in the costs of the product / service. Incremental innovation is widely used as sustaining competitive move, which helps the companies to enrich existing products or processes with new features, without incurring too much risk (Kingsland, 2007). Thus, incremental innovation is not about huge sweeping changes. On the contrary, companies that innovate incrementally tend to do so just a little bit at a time. Incremental innovation may, therefore, be seen as cost cutting or feature improvements in existing products or services (Leifer, 2000). In other words, companies that adopt this approach show dedication to continuous improvement in a way that meets market demands and keeps them relevant to the consumer. In the best case such a strategy will produce significant increases in sales, popularity, and enhance brand recognition. In the worst case the market simply would not respond to the product. Since the investment cost is relatively low, weak customer responses may not be catastrophic.

One of the most common examples of the incremental innovations cited in business textbooks is the early pentium chips developed by Intel. Pentium I up to Pentium IV were generally based on similar patterns. But each new version brought out newer technologies and innovations in their chipset. Another example is Google's release of Gmail, heralded by many as the best internet mail service. When Gmail was launched it had a limited feature set but did one thing very well, delivered emails. Unlike competitors it was clean and easy to use with no distracting flash ads and numerous interface improvements. Over time Google released more features and made the service better, faster, and easier to use.

From the above examples, it can be argued that an incremental innovation might involve optimisations of an existing structure or process – i.e. build upon existing knowledge and resources within a certain company. In this sense these innovations will be competence-enhancing. Some incremental innovation strategies now use open innovation and open source mechanisms to take advantage of the creativity of consumers and allegiances that they already have to a given product.

6.4 Internal Marketing Strategies

Following Ahmed and Rafiq (2011) internal marketing (IM) is a planned effort using a marketing-like approach directed at motivating employees, for implementing and integrating organizational strategies towards customer orientation. Employee motivation in this regard refers to the emotional commitment of employees to the attainment of organizational objectives. Similarly, Berry and Parasuraman (1991) argue that internal marketing enjoins managers to perceive their employees as internal customers. Thus, internal marketing is the task of hiring, training, retaining, motivating employees, and ensuring that the spirit of customer-consciousness guides every aspect of their professional life (Ballantyne, 1997). To succeed, internal marketing efforts require top management commitment, clearly communicated executive attitude to risk, management of conflicts to reduce tensions between and within departments, good reward systems and structures that encourage knowledge sharing and learning within organizations. These factors are briefly discussed in this section.

6.4.1 Top Management's Role

Top managers have the overall responsibility for the conduct and performance of organizations and therefore are pivotal in the understanding of what happens within any organization. Several studies of market orientation have pointed out that top management commitment to the development of market-oriented attitudes and the implementation of market-oriented activities enhances the degree of market orientation in the company (Egeren and O'Connor, 1998; Farrell, 2000; Celuch *et al.*, 2000; Conduit and Mavondo, 2001). Top managers' role is seen as that of creating context – through staffing, reward and measurement systems as well as culture and style – within which other employees work. Employees are expected to show greater commitment to learn when top management support is available, when they have training opportunities and when they are rewarded for the application of new knowledge to solve problems.

Managers differ by the extent to which they emphasize internal and external environmental factors in the process of collection, interpretation and utilization of information in marketing strategy

113

development and implementation. Internally-oriented managers are concerned with routinizing organisational activities such that greater efficiencies can be obtained. They rely predominantly on internal/organisational information, paying little attention to external market information. Externally-oriented managers do the reverse.

6.4.2 Management's Attitude to Risk

Top management risk orientation carries symbolic implications for organizational members' motivation to act (Brunsson, 2000). Following Kohli and Jaworski (1990), it can be argued that top management's willingness to take risks will encourage and facilitate organization-wide commitment to market orientation. On the other hand, a risk aversion policy adopted by senior management will tend to inhibit the process.

Furthermore, research has shown that management's attitudes to risk vary with culture (Hofstede, 1980). The tolerance for risk is found by Hofstede to be higher in North America and Northern Europe, while managers in Asian and African countries tend to avoid uncertainty. Although earlier studies found the impact of risk on market orientation not to be significant in the US (Jaworski and Kohli, 1993) and Scandinavia (Selnes *et al.,* 1996), Shoham and Rose (2001) suggested that its impact should be stronger in high uncertainty avoiding nations than in low uncertainty avoiding nations.

6.4.3 Inter-Departmental Conflict and Connectedness

Conflict situations are those in which one party perceives its interests to be negatively affected by another party. Antecedents of conflict include poor co-ordination, inadequate communication, unclear job boundaries, organizational complexity and incompatible personalities or value systems. Low level of conflict may strengthen the degree of inter-departmental connectedness. Task-related conflicts can, however, be constructive in the sense that they help people recognize problems, identify a variety of solutions and understand the issues involved. Conflicts can therefore improve team dynamics by strengthening their cohesiveness and task orientation when organizations face external threats.

Following Hofstede (1991) managers in different countries handle conflicts differently. Organizations located in low power distance countries tend to be more co-operative and show preference for consultative management style. Where high power distance prevails, employees tend to accept autocratic management styles as a mediator in inter-personal and inter-departmental conflicts. Furthermore, organizations located in individualistic cultures see conflict as healthy, on the basis that everyone has a right to express his views. People are encouraged to bring contentious issues into the open rather than suppress them. Collectivist cultures place greater value on social harmony and therefore discourage open confrontations.

6.4.4 Organizational Structure and Characteristics

Beker and Hombrug (1999) argue that a comprehensive analysis of a company's market orientation and the effect of its market-oriented behaviour must include the entire management system of the company. Management system in this regard should include the organization system, the information system, the planning system, the controlling system and the human resource management system. Organizations that have high levels of integration in terms of their values and norms tend to exhibit behavioural consistency across individuals and therefore facilitate the coordination of responsibilities among employees and departments (Davenport, 1993). Such organizations are described in the management literature as having strong cultures that convey a sense of identity to organizational members and facilitate the generation of commitment to something larger than the self. Widespread consensus and endorsement of organizational values and norms facilitates social control within an organization. When there is a broad agreement that certain behaviours are more appropriate than others, violations of behavioural norms may be detected and corrected faster, using informal social control mechanisms.

This, by implication means that the introduction of market oriented practices may necessitate the re-design of the company's structure, the re-allocation of its resources and the re-modelling of the company's information and communication networks (Avlonitis and Gounaris 1999). Organisational scholars have informed that the way information is used in organisations will be determined by the presence of organisational structures, systems and processes (Cyert and March, 1963; Daft and Weick, 1984). For example, the degrees of centralisation and formalisation of decision-making processes is seen as an attribute of organisational structures and systems. A company's ability to acquire, disseminate and utilise market information is shown to be inversely related to the degree of centralisation. This means decentralisation and informal organisational design tend to facilitate market-oriented behaviour. Decentralized structures permit flexibility and variety in the choice of knowledge acquisition methods as well as interpretations that organizational members bring to the information generated. In addition to this, interfunctional co-ordination entails the willingness of functional and divisional representatives of a company to listen to each other and to express their ideas honestly and openly (Lafferty and Hult, 1999).

6.4.5 Reward System

It has also been argued that the methods of performance appraisal and reward system applied in a company have been posited to impact on market orientation. Management evaluation systems and rewards tend to condition employees' motivation and learning (Salaman and Butler, 1990). Rewards reflect top management's perception of an individual's contribution to organizational goal attainment and condition individual behaviour.

To be motivating, reward systems must be seen by employees as fair, equitable and related to performance. A competency-based reward system, for example, indicates management's priority on the acquisition of skills and knowledge rather than task performance. It enables companies to satisfy variations and changes in their customers' needs since the requisite skills and knowledge for serving these needs exist within the company. The effectiveness of reward systems in motivating employees depends on the cultural values of the society within which the organization is located (Hofstede, 1980, 1991). Team-based reward systems are found to be effective in collectivist societies, but less so in individualist societies. In such societies, individual rewards create jealousies and competition among employees and therefore disrupt the collaboration needed for organizational learning.

6.4.6 Level of Job Satisfaction

Studies have also shown a positive link between employee's job satisfaction and their organizational commitment. Job satisfaction is seen by some scholars as a predictive variable in analysis of employees' desire to align their personal goals with those of their organizations (Shields and Ward, 2001). Meyers and Allen (1997) suggest that organizational commitment has three components that are not mutually exclusive: (1) *affective commitment* which is an emotional attachment to, identification with and involvement with the organization; (2) *continuance commitment*, representing an awareness of the costs associated with leaving the organization; and (3) *normative commitment*, indicating a feeling of obligation to continue to work for the organization. In other words, commitment may be triggered by a combination of these three conditions – i.e. desire, compulsion or obligation to work for the focal organization. Scholars such as Davenport (1993) and Loveman (1998) argue that commitment provides a basis for employees to engage in organization-supportive behaviours.

Furthermore, studies by Hackman and Oldham (1975, 1980) revealed that when jobs are designed with contents that allow employees to experience the psychological states of meaningfulness in their work, and if they have sufficient knowledge and skills to undertake the assignments, they tend to have strong positive feelings that will result in high levels of internal work motivation and job satisfaction. This will, in turn, raise their commitment to their work organizations.

6.5   Summary

Market-oriented businesses are usually described as being customer-centric – i.e. they see the customer as the king and seek to create superior value in order to provide maximum satisfaction to their target customers. That is, their strategies are in response to customer needs. They do so through two sets of activities: (1) response design (e.g. using market intelligence to develop plans), and (2) response implementation (e.g. executing such plans). The marketing literature has endorsed the understanding that companies must treat their employees as customers, and provide them with the skills, resources and authority to serve the external customers to the best of their ability. Highly motivated and committed employees are willing to go the extra mile to provide excitement to the customers of their companies.

References

Ahmed, Pervaiz K., and Rafiq, Mohammed (2011) *Internal Marketing Tools and concepts for Customer-focused Management* (Oxford:, Taylor & Francis)

Avlonitis, G.J. and Gounaris, S.P., (1999) "Marketing orientation and its determinants: an empirical analysis" *European Journal of Marketing* Vol. 33 No. 11 pp. 1003-1037

Ballantyne, D. (1997), "Internal networks for internal marketing", *Journal of Marketing Management*, Vol. 13, pp. 343-66.

Becker, Jan and Homburg, Christian (1999) "Market-oriented management: a system-based perspective" *Journal of Market Focused Management,* 4 pp. 17-41

Berry, L.L. and A. Parasuraman, (1991) *Marketing Service, Competing through Quality,* (New York, The Free Press)

Brunsson, N., (2000) *The irrational organisation* (Bergen: Fagbokforlaget)

Celuch, Kevin G., Kasouf, Chickery J., and Strieter, Jeffrey C. (2000) "The influence of organisational market orientation on individual-level market-oriented cognitions" *Psychology and Marketing* Vol. 17 No. 11 pp. 935-954

Conduit, Jodie and Mavondo, Felix T., (2001) "How critical is international customer orientation to market orientation?" *Journal of Business Research* 51 pp. 11-24

Cyert, R., and March, J. G., (1963) *A behaviour al Theory of the Firm* (Englewood Cliffs NJ: Prentice-Hall).

Daft, R.L. and Weick, K.E. (1984) "Toward a model of organisations as interpretations system" *Academy of Management Review* pp.284-95

Davenport, Thomas H., (1993) *Process Innovation –- Reengineering Work through Information Technology* (Boston, Harvard Business School Press)

Day, George S., (1994), "The Capabilities of Market-Driven Organizations," Journal of Marketing, 58 (October), 37–52.

Egeren, M.V., and O'Connor, S. (1998) "Drivers of market orientation and performance in service firms" *Journal of Service Marketing* Vol. 12 No. 1 pp. 39-58

Farrell, M.A. (2000) "Developing a Market-oriented Learning Organisation" *Australian Journal of Management* Vol. 25 No. 2 pp. 201-222

Jaworski, B.J and Kohli, A.K., (1993) "Market Orientation: Antecedents and Consequences" *Journal of Marketing* Vol. 57 pp. 53-70

Kingsland, B. (2007) *Proposal for new innovation measurement* (Washington, Department of Commerce. Economics and Statistics Administration)

Lafferty, B.A., and G.T.M. Hult, (2001) "A synthesis of contemporary market orientation perspectives" *European Journal of Marketing* Vol. 35 No. 1, 92-109

Leifer, Richard (2000) *Radical Innovation: How Mature Companies Can Outsmart Upstarts* (Boston, Harvard Business Press)

Loveman, Gary (1998), "Employee Satisfaction, Customer Loyalty and Financial Performance," *Journal of Service Research*, Vol.1No.1pp: 18-31.

Hackman, J. R., & Oldham, G. (1975) "Development of the job diagnostic survey" *Journal of Applied Psychology*, 60, 159-170

Hackman, J. R., & Oldham, G. R., (1980) *Work redesign* (Reading, MA: Addison-Wesley).

Hofstede, Geert (1980) *Culture's consequences: international differences in Work Related Values* (Beverly Hills: Sage Publications)

Hofstede, Geert (1991) *Cultures and organisations: software of the mind* (London: McGraw-Hill Book Company)

Meyer J and Allen N (1997), *Commitment in the Workplace: Theory, Research, and Application*, Sage Publications.

Narver, John C. and Slater, Stanley F., (1990) "The Effect of Market Orientation on Business Profitability" *Journal of Marketing*, Vol. 54 October pp. 20-35

Salaman, G., and Butler, J., (1990) "Why Managers Won't Learn" *Management Education and Development* Vol. 21 No. 3 pp: 183-191

Selnes, F.B., Jaworski, B.J and Kohli, A.K., (1996) "Market Orientation in United States and Scandinavian Companies: A Cross-Cultural Study" *Scandinavian Journal of Management* Vol. 12 No. 2 pp. 139-157

Shields, M.A., & Ward, M. (2001) "Improving nurse retention in the National Health Service in England: the impact of job satisfaction on intention to quit"*Journal of Health Economics*, 20, 677- 701

Shoham, A., and Rose, G. M. (2001) "Market Orientation: A Replication, Cross-National Comparison, and Extension" *Journal of Global Marketing*, Vol.14 No.4, pp: 5-14.

For Further Readings

Ferrell, O.C., Gonzalez-Padron, Tracy L., Hult, G. Tomas M. and Maignan, Isabelle (2010) "From Market Orientation to Stakeholder Orientation" *Journal of Public Policy & Marketing* Vol. 29 No.1 pp: 93–96

Homburg, Christian, Krohmer, Harley and Workman, John P., (2004) "A strategy implementation perspective of market orientation" *Journal of Business Research* Vol. 57 pp: 1331 – 1340

CHAPTER SEVEN

Relational Theories and Strategies in Marketing

7.1 Introduction

The notion that economic exchanges usually take place within complex multiparty contractual (or contract-like) relationships has been endorsed by the mainstream economic literature for nearly four decades now. Some scholars therefore see business activities within national, regional and global market place as being coordinates through a network of relationships. This thinking constitutes the core of what is now referred to as the network theory in business management. Following this perspective, markets are regarded as networks of connected interactions and relationships and not as atomic exchanges between buyers and sellers shaped by impersonal market forces of demand and supply.

The aim of this chapter is to review the stock of knowledge conveyed by relational theories and how they help us understand marketing activities. The discussions are initiated with a quick overview of neoclassical economic thinking with its emphasis on the market as resource allocative mechanism and the criticism of this perspective resulting in the formulation of the transactional cost theory. The section is followed by a discussion of the network theory (approach) to understanding supplier-buyer exchange relationships. This is followed by a review of international value chain and global commodity chain studies, the global production network studies, the strategic alliance studies, and relationship marketing studies each providing some contribution to what may be broadly classified as the relational theory of business. The final section brings together these discussions, focusing attention on the individual.

7.2 Pre-Relational Perspectives on Economic Exchanges

The general understanding in business economics is that companies require resources in order to produce goods and services that are earmarked for their customers. According to neoclassical microeconomics, companies secure their resources from the market and therefore engage in upstream transactions for this purpose. Each company is assumed to have maximisation of utility as its primary goal and maximum utility is defined in terms of prices. Thus market is seen as depending on price mechanisms to allocate resources. Companies depend on the market allocative mechanism when the benefits outweigh the costs of leaving it.

Microeconomic assumptions have, however, been criticised as being removed from reality and therefore providing inadequate conceptual framework and guide for understanding exchange structures and processes of companies. Following Williamson (1975), market transactions may become very costly due to two general factors: (1) behaviour-induced costs and (2) environment-induced costs. The behavioural-induced costs arise as a result of such factors as bounded rationality and opportunism. These combine with environmental factors such as uncertainty and structural constraints such as concentration and low resource mobility to raise overall operational costs. The exchange partners are normally assumed to behave intentionally in their interaction processes. It is argued that when partners can adopt robust contractual governing mechanism that build into their relationships sufficient incentives that hold their wilful self-interest seeking tendencies in check, they can engage in transactions on continual basis without the cost increasing consequences of opportunism and bounded rationality.

But contractual governance mechanisms are themselves cost-incurring. These include costs associated with information search, reaching a satisfactory agreement, relationship monitoring, adapting agreements to unanticipated contingencies and contract enforcement. Not only do companies incur costs in adopting contractual or supervisory (controlling) governance mechanisms, bounded rationality reduces the effectiveness of the control mechanism. It is for this reason that scholars of transaction costs economics advise against the reliance on markets (i.e. external governance mechanisms) under conditions of environmental instability and favour internalisation strategies such as vertical integration (i.e. internal governance mechanisms).

Although Transaction Costs Economics has provided useful insights into some of the factors that hamper exchanges in normal business practices, it has some fundamental conceptual weaknesses as well. One weakness lies in its preoccupation with the structure of relationships and reluctance to explicitly consider the possible dynamic evolutions of the relationships and the positive human tendencies that can override initial doubts, uncertainties and temptations for opportunism. As Morgan and Hunt (1994) argue, human behaviour in relationships is not as Machiavellian as described in transaction costs theory. It is in this light that the relational theories' contribution to marketing becomes important. One of the theories guiding this stream of research is the network theory.

7.3 The Network Approach

To network scholars business exchanges are not characterised by actions of sellers and reactions of buyers. Transactions are rather defined by interactions by active participants in the exchange relationship (Ford *et al.*, 1998). Through *networking* companies obtain access to important complementary assets, markets and technologies without incurring organisational or locational costs (which are typical of internal growth strategies), and free themselves from the limits of local (and internal) competence.

The network perspective shares with transaction costs economics the awareness that companies are resource dependent in the fulfilment of their underlying objectives. But while transaction costs economics doubts the ability of companies to secure the needed resources in a cost-efficient way through collaboration, this assumption lies at the core of the network approach. Borg (1991) argues that unlike transactional costs theory, an interactional approach places less emphasis on the cost of different forms of business relationships and more on the substance of the relationship. This shift, from the perception of the market as a means of exchange to its perception as interaction within and between organisations, has been dubbed by some scholars as a shift in paradigm (Borg, 1991; Grönroos, 1994).

The unit of focus and analysis in the network theory is the company. Companies select counterparts with which they sell products and exchange resources. They coordinate their relationships through interactions. Networks are found to be relatively stable because relationships take time and effort and therefore do not to change quickly. Relational bonds are identified to include technical, planning, knowledge, socio-economic and legal. These bonds are mainfestion in practice through product and process adjustments, logistical coordination, and knowledge about counterparts. In the words of Johanson and Mattsson (1987: 36) network relationships "are constantly being established, maintained, developed, and broken in order to give satisfactory, short-term economic returns and to create positions in the network that will assure the long-term survival and development of the company".

Participants in a network engage in by performing transformational and transactional activities. *Transformation activities* are those required within a company to add value to existing resources e.g. through production processes while transactional activities take place through exchanges. Series of activities within a network may come together to form a chain of transactions or may be loosely connected. To engage in these activities, network participants need resources. These may be grouped into three broad categories: financial, technological and human (including skills, knowledge and social ties). Combination of resources in a transformational process may produce efficiency and new knowledge. Activities and resources are therefore functionally interdependent.

A company's gain from a network relationship will depend on the power and knowledge structure of the network and the participant's position within this structure. Interactions with other network participants provide each participant with an opportunity to revise and redefine its needs and, in this way, find new possibilities within the network. This is referred to in the literature as the *interactive effect.*

Position is an important concept in the network theory. The theory draws on resource dependency theory to discuss the relative power of the exchange parties, based on their strategic vulnerability in the relationships. Companies occupy specific positions in the network. The position a company occupies at any given point in time is the outcome of own resources and previous activities combined with changes in external conditions and the company's resources. Current position again determines the possibilities of resource sharing with others within the network and future positions. Companies develop strategies that enable them to maintain favourable positions or move them into strategically advantageous positions. These strategies define each company's relationship with other companies.

The concept of position implies that companies undertake relationship-specific investments or what Johanson and Mattsson (1987) call "market assets".[1] Earlier studies of relational exchanges have paid limited attention to the social context within which these relationships take place. This omission has however been rectified by works of economic sociologists (Granovetter, 1985; Granovetter and Swederberg, 1992). These developments have influenced studies of internationalisation of companies.

Underlying the business exchange relationship is a process of social exchange. Network scholars appear to see social relationships as derivatives of business transactions, emerging automatically out of the successful transactions. That is, social relations need no extra efforts outside what is spent on business transactions. Thus in the view of Johanson and Mattsson (1987) each transaction provides partners with an opportunity to deepen their trust in each other and enables them to engage in major transactions in the future.

For network scholars, all businesses require network orientation in order to be successful. Having such an orientation encourages companies to identify the roles, strengths and resource configurations of other actors within the network. This helps them position themselves within the network. "Position" here is a rich term. By positioning themselves within the network of relationships, companies are able to design strategies that improve their access to resources controlled by other companies. The higher the number of contacts, the better it is for the company as this means access to more networks and providing their managers with greater access to opportunities.

7.4 Relationship Marketing

Another body of literature that contributes to relational theory in business is relationship marketing. The concept of relationship marketing (RM) has

---

[1] The concept of "market asset" is reminiscent of Williamson's (1985) concept of asset-specific investment.

been described as a new marketing paradigm, a new marketing strategy and an emerging school of marketing (Aijo, 1996). Crucial elements in the RM framework include interactivity, networking, trust, long term orientation and exchange of promises. As Shapiro *et al* (1995: 186) explain it, "relationship selling is not just a better set of techniques for making sales. It is a different philosophy based upon continuity and trust". Concepts such as symbiotic marketing, co-marketing alliances, internal marketing are now widely used in the literature to explain the characteristics of relationship marketing.

Several factors have contributed to the importance of RM in current business practices. They include the general affluence in the Western industrialised economies, globalisation, technological innovations, information revolutions (computer and telecommunication developments) all of which have combined to produce a buyer's market characterised by limitless buyer choices. These circumstances have compelled companies to simultaneously raise efficiency through cost minimisation and improve the level of quality of their products. Quality expectations of customers everywhere have increased. To serve them, vendors must have up-to-date awareness of the expectations their current and potential customers and work with them to succeed.

From international industrial marketing perspective, this requirement implies that suppliers must either be located in close proximity to customers and/or strengthen their connectivity through the use of Internet technology. It has also been noted that successful relationships between suppliers and customers require the broader involvement of organisational actors in the collaborating companies, i.e. pulling together knowledge, commitment and trust from many people.

Companies engaged in relationship marketing must therefore be mindful of the fact that relationships involve a substantial loss of autonomy. Evidently, this understanding of inter-company relationship leans on the earlier theories outlined above, namely transaction costs economics, network theory and international value chain theory.

Following Aijo (1996) the entry of relationship on the centre stage of marketing theory can be traced along two parallel routes. First, there was a growing emphasis on customer relationships within the service industries in the 1970s and 1980s. This was partly due to the spate of deregulations within the industry leading to intensive competition and situations in which competitors "snatched" customers from each other. Under these conditions keeping one's existing customers (as opposed to winning new customers) was deemed to be a useful strategy. Parallel to this development, business-to-business marketers realised that the service components of their product offerings (i.e. repairs, maintenance, delivery, training etc.) were critical to the satisfaction of their customers (Groönroos, 1994). Performing these tasks necessitated keeping and coordinating relationships with multiple sets of actors. Thus although the concept of "relationship marketing" was not explicitly adopted in the business-to-business marketing of the 1970s, it certainly constituted a central component of its strategies.

A review of the history of marketing thoughts and theory also indicate that the notion of relationship has always been an underlying guiding principle. Marketing is presented by Sheth *et al*, (1988) as a study of the behaviour of buyers, sellers, intermediaries and regulators in exchange relationships with an emphasis on understanding the processes of the interaction. The term "marketing concept" was introduced early in the marketing literature to mean "customer orientation", whereby relationship with customers was considered as a key determinant of a company's performance. In the 1990s, the marketing concept has been revived in marketing research under the concept of market orientation. It is therefore argued that "buyer-seller relationship" must not be conceived as a binary construct but as a continuum (Hausman, 2001; Grönroos, 1990). This understanding means, in effect, that every exchange has an element of relationship, although some of them may be richer in relationship than others.

Building on this understanding, Huasman (2001) introduces the concept of "relationship strength" to reflect differences in the relational character of business relationships. She defines relationship strength as ties between relational partners reflecting their ability to weather both internal and external challenges to the relationship. She argues then that relationship strength would depend on the levels of trust and commitment between focal business partners. The emphasis on trust and commitment as definitional constituents of relationship strength is consistent with several other studies in the contemporary literature on business relationships (See Morgan and Hunt, 1994).

7.5 Trust and Relationships in Marketing

Trust is widely recognised as a critical component in successful relationship marketing. In the social science literature, trust is believed to be that social attribute that generates a willingness among people in dyadic relations to sacrifice their short-run individual self-interests for the attainment of joint goals or longer-term objectives (Sabel, 1993). People who trust each other believe that their relationships are worth sustaining and therefore actively contribute to its continuity. That is, trust leads to higher levels of loyalty and long-term collaboration between people (Fukuyama, 1995).

Similar perspectives are reflected in the industrial marketing literature. Anderson and Narus (1990 p.45) define trust as "the company's belief that another company will perform actions that result in positive outcomes for the company, as well as not take unexpected actions that would result in negative outcomes for the company". Trust allows companies to reduce or avoid reliance on costly formal monitoring mechanisms to maintain their partnership. It also produces mutual concern for longer term benefits by partners, raises market performance through the improvement of efficiency, and allows for information exchange, joint problem solving attitude and mutual learning (Aulakh, Kotabe and Sahay, 1996). Furthermore, trust complements written contracts between companies. A contract cannot be expected to address every eventuality and contingency faced over the course of a long-term relationship. Where trust exists between the partners they will adapt to unanticipated contingencies without resorting to opportunism. As Sabel (1993) observes, trust requires a mutual suspension of self-interest of the interacting partners. That is, it lays the foundation for a mutual confidence among business partners that no party to an exchange will exploit the other's vulnerability. Universal suspicion is therefore replaced by shared confidence.

Trust between cross-national partners requires cultural sensitivity. The argument here is that cultural sensitivity promotes regular and effective communication between the collaborating companies and thereby reduces the incidence of misunderstanding and suspicion. Trust is therefore seen as a culture-dependent concept since the underlying logics of trust differ across societies. For example, Johnson, Cullen, Sakano and Takenouchi, (1996) found a wide discrepancy between Japanese and Western ideas of trust. They further noted that the rules of trust building observed by partners based in the same culture differ from those observed by partners belonging to different cultures.

Relationship marketing has its challenges. It can result in relationship-specific investments. As the transaction costs theory informs, these are specialised investments that partners make that are of little value outside the specific vendor-buyer relationship due to their idiosyncratic nature. For example, a vendor who devotes its engineering expertise to solve a unique design problem for a manufacturer has made a relationship-specific investment. At least, in the short run, the vendor's investment is neither easily transferred nor recovered if the relationship terminates. Thus, the more relationship-specific investment partners make the more dependent they become on each other.

Exit barriers also constitute a negative dimension of relationship marketing. Exit barriers are said to be present in a relationship when partners believe that terminating established relationships would be costly. The more difficult it is to gain access to the resources supplied by the other party to a relationship, the more dependent a company is to the relationship. When avenues exist to gain the same resources (in terms of quality, delivery reliability and post-sales support) the more likely it is for partners to pull away from the relationship.

Morgan and Hunt (1994) have therefore suggested that *commitment* and *trust* should be considered the foundations of a supplier-customer relationship. The committed party believes the relationship is worth working on and therefore actively contributes to its continuity. Commitment is built on trust, i.e. confidence in each other's reliability and integrity. Trust therefore leads to higher levels of loyalty. "When both commitment and trust - not just one or the other - are present", they argue, "they produce outcomes that promote efficiency, productivity and effectiveness" (Morgan and Hunt, 1994, P.22).

In international marketing, relationship marketing has manifested itself in the mode of operations and the degree of internationalisation. Needs of foreign customers must be understood and adequately fulfilled through real time deliveries of required goods and services and by collaboration to develop customized solutions. Relationship with local companies has been suggested as a preferable mode of entry into new markets (particularly distant markets) because it helps reduce the liability of foreignness. Through such relationships foreign partners can capitalize on local partners' locational and reputational resources (Hausman, 2001). This resource sharing reduces overall cost of market entry and provides opportunities for more rapid market knowledge acquisition.

7.6 The Role of Individuals in International Intercompany Relations

Contemporary relational theories in business studies appear to have ignored an explicit articulation of the role of the individual in the governance of exchange relationships. A quote from Johanson and Mattsson (1987:40) reveals the standpoint of the network theory on this issue:

> We have discussed intercompany relationships without explicitly referring to individual actors. However, the mutual orientation among companies is principally a mutual orientation among individual actors in those companies. In some cases the mutuality is primarily a matter of interpersonal relationships between salesmen and purchasers; in other cases, a number of persons on different levels and with different specialisations may be mutually oriented towards each other. Correspondingly, the interaction processes are carried out by individuals – *though we have discussed them as taking place among companies* (p 40). Emphasis added.

Despite this awareness the authors stated that the characteristics of the relationships are determined by structural circumstances. The possibilities of changing relationships through individual decisions are given limited attention. If we accept the argument that people make decisions and carry them through in every organization, then individual decision makers must be explicitly considered in all business relationship theories. Without explicitly factoring the individual into our models of intercompany relationships we have an incomplete basis for understanding what drives the outcomes (positive or negative) of such relationships. This is particularly true for international business relations where uncertainties due to geographical divide and risk of opportunism may make decision makers hesitant to make commitments that are vital for success. This is why companies do send their staff overseas to negotiate deals and to supervise specific aspects of contracted collaborations. People "on the spot" are able to register errors of interpretation of ideas and thoughts conveyed and rectify them quickly enough to avoid misunderstandings that may sow the seed of mistrust between companies. Thus, top managers must acknowledge the role of the individual in the management of inter-company relations and must consciously encourage individuals to play this role, especially in cross-national intercompany relationships.

In international business context, in particular, where there is a geographical distance between companies and their customers or suppliers, it is the resident representatives of the companies (as individuals) that carve the image of the companies within the local networks. That is, the behaviour of the representatives shapes the identities of their companies and determines the degree of trust and social support that the companies can count on within the local operational environment (Baker, 2001). In the words of Adams (1976, p.1175), the individual plays a "boundary-spanning role for the company".

The concept of *personal bonding* (Williams *et al.*, 1998) has been introduced into the literature to characterise the individual's role in inter-company relations. This is in contrast to structural bonding that characterises organisation-specific relationships. Personal bonding defines the personal and social relationships that individuals in one company have with their counterparts in another company. These bonds contribute immensely to the stability and predictability of the relationships. Jackson (1985) suggests that in industrial marketing and outsourcing situations buyers may tend to depend on the personal representatives of their sellers as a guarantee for the reliability of the information and business value delivered to them.

Social psychologists argue that individuals' personal intentions towards each other and their perceptions of each other influence the intensity of their relationships. People tend to make relationship-specific investments such as emotional commitments to relationships that mean much to them personally or to their career and social mobility. They see these emotional investments as pledges for collaboration (Anderson and Weitz, 1992). If these individuals are key representatives of their respective organisations, the personal relationships invariably define the relationships between organisations. Over time, idiosyncratic investments are expected to transform an economic exchange into a socially embedded relationship (Campbell, 1997). When individuals within companies understand and appreciate each other's viewpoints, they are able to arrive at a working consensus and manage the relationship between their companies more effectively. In this relationship management process, individuals are guided partly by socially prescribed expectations and rules of accepted behaviours (Granovetter and Swedberg, 1992; Heide and John, 1992). These social norms or principles act as control mechanisms to coordinate the activities performed by the individuals (Campbell, 1997).

7.6 Summary

In sum, relational theories in business address the issues of inter-company exchanges and governance of resources and value creating activities. The received understanding is that these exchanges and activities take place at multiple levels both within the companies (i.e. by way of internalisation and internal marketing), but more particularly in companies' external network of relationships.

It is plausible to argue that the relationship theoretical framework captures what businesses have been doing for centuries. What has happened in the 1990s can be described as an academic discovery of what has existed and is vigorously practised for years. The fact that an increasing number of companies are engaged in various forms of linkages – outsourcing, co-sourcing, strategic alliances etc. – attest to the durability of relational thinking in business management.

References

Aijo, Toivo S. (1996) "The theoretical and philosophical underpinnings of relationship marketing" *European Journal of Marketing* Vol.30 No.2: 8-18

Anderson, James C. and James A. Narus (1990), "A Model of Distributor Firm and Manufacturer Firm Working Partnerships", *Journal of Marketing*, 54 (January), 42-58.

Anderson, E. and Weitz, B (1992) "The use of pledges to build and sustain commitment in distribution channels" *Journal of Marketing Research* Vol. 12 No. 6: 18-34

Aulakh, P. S., Kotabe, M., & Sahay, A. (1996). Trust and performance in cross-border marketing partnerships: A behaviour al approach. *Journal of International Business Studies*, (Special Issue), Vol. 27 No.5pp: 1005-1032

Baker, Tim (2001) "Customer-focused organizations: Challenges for managers, workers and human resource practitioners" *Journal of Management Development* Vol. 21 No. 4: 306-314

Borg, Erik A. (1991)"Problem shifts and market research: the role of networks in business relationships" *Scandinavian Journal of Management* Vol.7 No.4: 285-295

Cambell, Alexandra (1997) "Buyer-supplier partnerships: flip sides of the same coin" *Journal of Business and Industrial Marketing* Vol.12 No. 6: 417-434

Ford, D. (Ed.) (1990) *Understanding Business Markets: Interaction, relationship and networks* London Academic Press Limited

Ford, D., Gadde, L., Håkansson, H., Lundgren, A., Snehota, I., Turnbull, P. and Wilson, D. (1998) *Managing Business Relationships* Chichester: John Wiley and Sons

Fukuyama, F. (1995): *Trust. The Societal Virtues and the Creation of Prosperity* (New York, Free Press)

Granovetter, Mark (1973), "The Strength of Weak Ties." *American Journal of Sociology* 78(6): 1360- 1380.

Granovetter, M. S. (1985), "Economic Action and Social Structure: The Problem of Embeddedness", *American Journal of Sociology*, 91, 3, pp. 481-510.

Grönroos, Christian (1990) *Service management and marketing: Managing the moments of truth in service competition* Lexington MA Lexington Books

Grönroos, Christian (1994) "From marketing mix to relationship marketing: towards a paradigm shift in marketing" *Management Decision* Vol. 32 No.2: 4-20

Hausman, Angela (2001) "Variations in relationship strength and its impact on performance and satisfaction in business relationships" *Journal of Business and Industrial Marketing* Vol.16 No. 7: 600-616

Johanson, Jan and Mattsson, Lars-Gunnar (1987) "Inter-organisational relations in industrial systems: A network approach compared with the transaction-cost approach" *International Studies of Management and Organisation*Vol. 17 No. 1: 34-48

Morgan, Robert M; Hunt, Shelby D (1994) "The commitment-trust theory of relationship marketing" *Journal of Marketing* 58, 3; pp: 20

Mowery, D., Oxley, J.E., and Silverman, B., (1996) "Strategic Alliance and Business-to-business Knowledge Transfer" *Strategic Management Journal* 17 (4): 77-91

Sabel, Charles F., (1993) "Studied Trust: Building New Forms of Co-operation in a Volatile Economy" *Human Relations* Vol. 46 N0.9 pp: 1133-1170

Weitz, Barton A. and Sandy D. Jap (1995) "Relationship Marketing and Distribution Channels" *Journal of the Academy of Marketing Science* 23 (4): 305-320.

Williams, Jerome D., Han, Sang-Lin, and Qualls, William J., (1998) "A conceptual model and study of cross-cultural business relationship" *Journal of Business Research* 42, 135-143

Williamson, O. E., (1975) *Markets and Hierarchies: Analysis and Antitrust Implications* (The Free Press)

For Further Readings

Aulakh, Peter S, Kotabe, Massaki and Sahay, Arvind (1996) "Trust and Performance in Cross-Border Marketing Partnerships: "Behavioural

Approach", *Journal of International Business Studies* Vol. 27 No.5 pp: 1005-1032.

Coleman, James S. (1988) "Social Capital in the Creation of Human Capital" *American Journal of Sociology* Vol. 94 Supplement pp: 95-120

Portes, Alejandro (1998), 'Social Capital: Its Origins and Applications in Modern Sociology', *Annual Review of Sociology*, Vol. 24 No. 1 pp: 1-24

Samiee, S. and Walters, P.G., (2003) "Relationship Marketing in an International Context: A Literature Review" *International Business Review* Vol. 12 No. 2 pp: 193-214

Wilson, David T. (1995). "An Integrated Model of Buyer-Seller Relationships" *Journal of the Academy of Marketing Science* 23 (4): 335-345.

CHAPTER EIGHT

Organizational Buying Behaviour and Strategies

8.1 Introduction

The concept of organisational or industrial marketing is used to describe marketing activities targeted at all individuals and organisations that acquire products and services that are used in the production of other products and services. These products include capital goods (e.g. buildings, land and machines), operational products (e.g. accessory equipment, supplies, maintenance services), and output products (e.g. raw materials, components, production services). The justification for creating industrial marketing as a specific field of study in marketing derives from the awareness that the market behaviour, which affects the demand and purchases of industrial products and services, is generally different from that experienced in consumer markets.

One of the distinctive differences between industrial and consumer markets is that the demand for industrial products is a *derived demand*, meaning that the magnitude of demand for these products varies with the demand for the finished products and services based on them. The purchasing process of industrial products is also relatively more complex, and may be divided into a number of stages taking place over time. The purchase decision making process usually involves many people who are drawn from different departments of the buying organisation, depending on the strategic importance of the products or services being purchased. In contrast to consumer markets, industrial products are funded with organisational resources. That is, the buyers of industrial products do not finance the purchase with their personal money, but rather use organisational funds for the purpose. This chapter introduces some of the fundamental concepts and models that describe and guide the decision making processes of buyers and vendors in the industrial market.

8.2 Factors Influencing the Buying Process

Three groups of factors influence industrial buying process, (1) the environment, (2) the organisation, and (3) the decision-making unit. The environment in this regard covers government regulations, the economic climate within which the buyers operate, and the general technological changes within the economy. In the increasingly globalised economies of today, buying processes must take factors other than the domestic environmental changes into account in their purchasing decision. Changes elsewhere in the world must also be factored into the purchase decision process. The international environment is in fact assuming greater importance than the domestic environment of most firms. The organisational structure, politics and culture also shape the manner in which purchase decisions are made. Finally, the decision-making unit (the buying centre) to which the purchasing task has been assigned also has a tremendous influence on the purchase process.

There are three groups of buyers at which industrial marketers target their products. These are (1) manufacturers, (2) intermediate customers, and (3) public institutions. Manufacturers usually buy raw materials, components, and finished items that they use in the manufacture of final goods. These customers tend to be geographically concentrated (e.g. in industrial area/zones of a country), buy in relatively larger quantities and their purchasing decisions are taken by a selected number of people. These characteristics make it relatively easier for a vendor to serve them compared with serving final consumers. Intermediate customers are channel members or resellers. They buy and sell to make profit. Some make changes to the products they sell (e.g. repackage them). Thus, an export company or a distributor is an intermediate customer whose purchase decisions are influenced by the demand of the customers that they serve. Public institutions such as schools, hospitals, prisons, the military and public offices constitute a major category of buyers of industrial products. The annual budgets of some public bodies in the developed countries can be a multiple of the expenditure of private sector organisations.

Unlike many consumers, manufacturers usually demand that the products they buy meet strict standards. Thus, when making a purchase, they tend to consider multiple benefits the product offers, particularly how it will perform. They may therefore contract their suppliers to design products to meet specifications they need. This means customization may be an important marketing strategy when selling to manufacturers.

The intermediate buyer is typically interested in whether the product is helping to achieve organizational goals and therefore less concerned with whether a product works as advertised. Some intermediate buyers may negotiate with suppliers on certain product matters such as packaging – larger intermediate buyers may require that the product be provided in certain package sizes or designs.

In most countries, however, most public sector purchasing is through tenders. Three tendering procedures can be identified, each with a different level of publicity of the tender notice:

1. *Open tendering,* where the invitation to tender is given the widest publicity;
2. *Selective tendering*, where the invitation is restricted to a predetermined list of suppliers,
3. *Private contracting*, where the awarding authority contacts suppliers individually to make a tender.

Contracts may be awarded on the basis of the following criteria

1. *Automatic tendering*, where the contract is awarded on the basis of a predetermined criterion such as the lowest bid, or some other criterion either in isolation or in conjunction with price
2. *Discretionary tendering*, in which the contract is awarded to the bid that is assessed to be most advantageous to the buying authority. The criteria are not pre-determined.
3. *Negotiated tendering*, in which the awarding authority negotiates freely with the supplier

8.3 International Dimensions of Industrial Marketing

As noted in chapter seven, global competitiveness has necessitated the use of inter-firm collaborative arrangements as a means of sustaining the competitive advantages of firms. Close relations between suppliers and buyers allow them to acquire new technical skills or technological capabilities. Interfirm relations can take a wide variety of forms. They include simple vendor – customer exchanges where the collaboration is restricted to the transfer of the contracted technology and knowledge, to joint ownership and development arrangements (Mowery, Oxley and Silverman, 1996).

The increasing cross-national vendor-buyer relations have also been reflected in the increasing use of contract production and outsourcing of inputs in different parts of the world. This is combined with the increasing demand for technology capacity enhancement packages in the emerging market economies of the world as well as the increasing demand by governments and multilateral public bodies of goods and services to extend the international dimensions of industrial marketing. These developments have also brought into focus problems of doing business across disparate cultural and business systems. The differences of the operational environments of existing customers that have internationalised their business as well as local businesses located in diversified environments cannot be ignored if firms would wish to sustain their competitiveness within the current dynamic global environment.

Alongside these developments, it has been noted that the philosophy of total quality management has caught up very fast within the global manufacturing sector and has enabled firms to reduce production cycle times and maintain zero inventories. This strategy again requires close collaboration between suppliers and buyers of industrial goods. The interaction between companies has been greatly facilitated in recent years through advances in information technology, particularly the increasing usage of Internet facilities as well as the establishment of regional economic blocks.

8.4 The Buy Grid Model

Industrial buyers are reputed for making rational decisions and go through a number of clearly defined stages in their decision-making. The purchase behaviour that they exhibit and the kind of information they require to make their decisions will depend on the experience of the decision-makers with the purchase of the same or similar products. The stages in the decision making process and the influence of the purchase situations on the decisions are described in the literature by a model referred to as *buygrid model*. Furthermore, organisational buying decisions are usually made by a group of organisational members labelled in the marketing literature as a *buying centre*. This chapter provides an overview of the buygrid model and the buying centre concept.

The buygrid model is a conceptual model, which describes the different combinations of buying phases and buying situations. This classification is built on three dimensions: the degree of novelty of the tasks to be carried out to reach a final decision on the purchase, the need for information and the number of alternatives considered. Taking these factors into consideration, the authors distinguish between the following three situations or types of purchase: straight rebuy, modified rebuy and new task buy. The model proposed by Robinson *et al.* (1967) is still useful for identifying participants in the buying process, specifying the circumstances under which an individual participates and determining the influence of each participant. This model incorporates three types of buying situations and describes the different combinations of buying phases and buying situations. The three buying situations are as follows:

1. The new tasks situation,
2. The modified re-buy situation
3. The straight re-buy situation

8.4.1 New Tasks Situation

It is a buying situation in which the business buyer purchases a product or service for the first time. In a new task buying situation the buyer seeks a wide variety of information to explore alternative solutions to his purchasing problem. The greater the cost or perceived risks related to the purchase the greater the need for information and the larger the number of participants in the decision making unit. This provides the vendor with considerable opportunity and challenge. The vendor is in a greater position to influence the decision making process by the information that it provides. At the same time its personnel must respond to the information needs and scepticism of a large number of people within the decision-making unit.

8.4.2 Modified Rebuy

It is a buying situation in which the business buyer wants to replace a product or service that the firm has been using. The decision making may involve plans to modify the product specifications, prices, terms or suppliers. This is the case when managers of the company believe that significant benefits such as quality improvement or cost reduction can be achieved by making the change. The fact that the company had previous experience with the purchase and use of the product means that the decision criteria may be well defined in such situations. Nevertheless, some uncertainties still linger in the minds of some decision-makers. There is the risk that the new supplier may perform poorer than the present one. Again the situation carries enormous opportunities and challenges for vendors competing for the order. The decision making unit is however usually smaller than in new task situation and therefore makes it relatively easier for the vendor's marketing personnel to attend effectively to the information needs of the buyers.

Take the example of a law firm that wants to improve its IT resources to maximize productivity and streamline operations to increase caseload capacity due to the influx of new clients. It will ask a team within the firm to review the effectiveness of its current IT solutions, redefine its needs, modify the service specifications and criteria for selecting service suppliers. The fact that the company had previous experience with the purchase and use of the service means that the decision criteria may be well defined in such situations. Nevertheless, some uncertainties may still linger in the minds of some decision-makers. The challenge you face in a modified re-buy situation is to convince your potential customer that by selecting you, the company will receive greater value than from the previous service provider.

8.4.3 Straight Rebuy Situation

It is a buying situation in which the buyer routinely re-orders a product or service without any modification due to satisfaction with the supplier. The supplier is retained as long as the level of satisfaction with the delivery, quality and price is maintained. New suppliers can only be considered if these conditions change. The challenge for the new supplier then is to offer better conditions or draw the buyer's attention to some benefits that it is missing for doing business with its present supplier. The buyer may in turn use the new offerings from competitors to renegotiate its purchase conditions with the present supplier. It is therefore difficult to capture orders from companies engaged in routine purchases.

Buun (1993) argues that the business buying situations are more complex than is generally considered in the existing literature. He has therefore suggested an additional classification of each of the three buying situations. The thrust of his argument is that the behaviour that buyers exhibit in each of the situations will depend on how strategic the purchase is for the company. Figure 8.1 provides an overview of the three buying situations and the decisional characteristics related to them.

Figure 8.1 The Three Task Situations

Decision Situational Characteristics	Purchase Situations and Behaviour					
	New Task		Modified Rebuy		Straight Rebuy	
	Strategic	Judgmental	Simple	Complex	Casual	Routine (Low Priority)
Degree of task Uncertainty	Moderate	High	Low	Low	Low	Moderate
Purchase importance	Very high	Very high	Quite high	Very high	Minor	Somewhat important
Extensiveness of choice set	Narrow	Very narrow	Narrow	Much choice	Very extensive	Much
Perceived buyer power	Strong	Moderate	Moderate	Strong	Little or none	Moderate
Behavioural Profile	High level of info. search *Great deal of of analysis * No previous guidelines *Limited opportunity to control purchase process	Moderate amount of info. search, analysis and proactive focusing * No previous guidelines	Moderate amount of info. search and analysis * High level of proactive behaviour * Follow standard procedures	Seemingly rational behaviour * Great deal of info. search & analysis * Focus on long term needs and supply reliability * Closely follow established procedures	No info. search and analysis * No proactive behaviour	Limited info. search and analysis * Limited proactive behaviour * Follow standard rules and procedures

Adapted from Bunn (1993) p. 47

8.5. Phases in the Purchase Decision Process

Conventionally, business purchase decisions are expected to go through a set of phases. Purchases in new task situations go through eight phases, the number of phases and their relative importance decreases in the case of the other purchase situations.

Phase 1: Anticipation or Recognition of a Problem (Need)
In rational purchase situations, the purchase decision will be triggered by the buying organisation's recognition of a need, problem or potential opportunity to gain new benefits within the changing environment. The trigger may be either external (e.g. new information from a potential supplier), or internal (e.g. an awareness of declining efficiency due to outmoded technology). This is a phase in the purchase decision process during which the information a vendor provides is critical since the buyer is in wide search of solutions to the problem identified.

Phase 2: Determination of the Characteristics and Quality of the Needed Items
Having acknowledged the problem, the next stage is to explore alternative solutions. It may be decided to solve the problem in a novel manner, i.e. exploring technical solutions unfamiliar with the buyer- a new task situation. Alternatively management may decide to find a modified/improved version of solutions with which they have been familiar – modified rebuy situation. Questions such as "what application requirements must be emphasised" and "what performance specifications should be used in evaluating in coming proposal" receive attention in this phase. The department whose staff is the users of the product is prominent at this stage. Their suggestions receive serious attention. Prospective suppliers are therefore advised to examine the information needs of the users and provide it to them to enable them make the choices that favour their products.

Phase 3: Description of the Characteristics and Quality of the Needed Items & Phase 4: Search for and Qualification of Potential Sources
Having specified the characteristics that buyers should look for, the market is then scanned for the products that fit these characteristics and the quantities to buy. If a supplier has contributed information to the first phase, that supplier will be certainly consulted to advise the buyer on where to get the best products. If the supplier has the product in question

within its product line, it is placed in a lucky position of influencing the choice decision. It may suggest modifications of its own product to fit the specific needs of the buyer. It has been shown that such partnering relationship with a buyer is highly advantageous in new task situations.

Phase 5: Acquisition and Analysis of Proposals

In this phase, qualified vendors are contacted with a request to make product offerings that can address the buyer's problem. In straight rebuy situations, the existing vendor will be the only supplier that the buyer will contact. For modified rebuy situations, there will be the need to analyse incoming proposals carefully before a final decision is made. The analysis of proposals becomes even more elaborate in new task situations.

Phase 6: Evaluation of Proposals and Selection of Suppliers

The decision-making unit carefully compares the various offers in terms of the criteria decided upon earlier. A few of the proposals are selected and the purchaser is authorised to initiate negotiations with the vendors concerned. Where the differences between the proposals are not pronounced, personal taste and considerations indirectly enter the decision making process.

Phase 7: Selection of an Order Routine

Order is placed with the selected vendor and the delivery as well as payment conditions are specified. For some types of machines and equipment, the delivery may also include installation and training of users. Here again the users' voices become very important since their evaluation is important in determining how successful the purchase has been.

Phase 8: Performance and Feedback Evaluation

This is the phase in which the performance of the product in matched against the expectations of the buyer in order to determine the gap, if any between them. As noted above, the evaluation of the users carries a heavy weight in the overall assessment of the performance of the vendor.

8.6 The Buying Centre Concept

Companies do not buy, people do. It is therefore important to have a substantial knowledge about those involved in the buying decision making process of the goods and/or services that a vendor intends to sell. It has been shown that many individuals are involved in the buying processes of industrial goods. Marketers gradually became aware of the significance of the buying center: the group of people belonging to different departments of the organization who participate and influence in the buying process (Robinson *et al.*, 1967; Webster and Wind, 1972; Sheth, 1973; Choffray and Lilien, 1980; Osmonbekov, Bello and Gilliland, 2002). It is especially important for marketing managers to identify the members that participate and influence in the buying center during the decision-making process. They can thereby avoid wasting their marketing efforts, especially in terms of communication, on irrelevant individuals, and instead concentrate their efforts on the most influential members.

The theoretical foundation of the buying centre construct can be found in role theory. Role theory suggests that people behave with a set of norms or expectations that others have in the roles in which they have been placed. Roles can be both formal and informal. Formal roles are defined by organisational structure and managers' position within the structure. Apart from the formal roles that managers play, they (like all other people) have the natural tendency to develop informal social groupings within their organisations. These informal groupings can be harnessed to support the performance of the main tasks that have been assigned to them. Occasionally, however, some informal social relations can obstruct the performance of these tasks.

There are two other important dimensions of the buying centre that require attention, the vertical dimension and the horizontal dimension. The vertical dimension refers to how many layers of management are involved in the purchase decision process. The horizontal dimension concerns the number of departments involved. The more complex a purchase decision, the wider both the horizontal and vertical coverage of the buying centre. It implies that individuals with a wide variety of interests and departments with different norms and rules of behaviour are involved in the process. This may create problems of co-ordination and may produce conflicting decision signals to the vendor.

8.6.1 The Roles of Buying Centre Members

Buying managers are known to assume some common roles in a buying process. These roles are classified into the following six groups:

1. Initiator
2. Gatekeeper
3. Influencer
4. Decider
5. Purchaser
6. User

The initiator is the person or group of individuals who become aware of a company's problem and recognises that the problem can be solved via acquisition of a product or service. Gatekeepers usually act as problem or product experts. They have information about a range of service provider offerings. Other buying centre members therefore rely on their information for their assessment of prospective service providers' offerings. Thus, by controlling information, and, by having access to decision-makers in the firm, the gatekeepers largely determine which service providers get the chance to sell. Influencers have been described as those who have a say in whether a product or service should be bought or not. The more critical a purchase is to a company's business, the higher the number of influencers. Critically, strategic purchases frequently entail high resource outlays and affect the task performance of several employees the heads of whom naturally "have a say" in the purchase decision making process. The deciders actually make the purchase decision. That is, they say yes or no to each service provider's offer. In less complex purchase situations, the decision-making responsibility may fall on one person. But where the purchase is complex, group decision may be required. The purchaser is the one who makes arrangements for the delivery of the goods. He is also often directly involved in negotiating the conditions under which the transactions will be made. The users are those who actually make use of the services in a normal working process.

A buying centre can be formalised, but not always so. Even in formalised buying centres, members are not designated with the titles of gatekeepers, influencers etc. A buying centre member may play more than one role at different stages in the buying process. There may be as few as one person playing all the six roles or as many as 50 or more in complex buying situations. The degrees of influence of these buying centre members will depend on their power base within the organisation.

One major characteristic of buying centres is that members come and go. The centre is, therefore, fragmented in terms of time. Some buying centre members are involved for only short periods of time in the purchase decision making process. If this happens the buying centre becomes even more fragmented over time. This means that the influence of key buying centre members can be limited to a particular stage in the purchasing process. It is, therefore, of utmost importance to service providers to exert the best impact on them at the critical point in time to convince them of the superior value of their offerings.

8.6.2 Buyers' Perception of Vendors

Buyers carry different perceptions about vendors, based on some previous encounters with them or information received about them from external sources. For most large organizations, the perceptions of their buying centres depend on two interrelated factors: (i) perception of the offerings made by the prospective vendor, and (ii) their perception of the vendor's organisation and its salespeople. It is therefore prudent for vendors to be aware of how potential buyers perceive them prior to making any sales effort.

Product and service attributes that have been found to influence customers' perception of the offerings include quality, reliability, post-delivery arrangements, price, and conditions of payment. Similarly customers' perception of the vendor's salespeople will be based on the criteria such as reliability, credibility, responsiveness, product knowledge, persuasiveness, knowledge about competitors, oral communication, personal charm/friendship as well as mutual trust and respect.

Although overall buying centre perception of the vendor is useful it is equally important to assess each buying centre member's perception of the vendor. This will help the vendor's sales people to plan their marketing efforts. The reasons why a specific buying centre member has a negative perception of the vendor must be thoroughly analysed and steps taken to correct any possible misunderstanding that might have produced the negative perception.

8.6.3 Uncertainties and Information Requirement of Buying Centre Members

Buying centre members need information in order to reduce one or more of the following three types of uncertainty.

Need uncertainty
Need uncertainty arises when the buying centre members doubt the nature of needs that the vendor's offerings are to satisfy. The general view is that buyers have clear knowledge of the problems that new products to be purchased are to address. In practice, however, not all the buying centre members are likely to be convinced about the nature of the problem and the type of solutions suggested. The reason may be due to lack of technical knowledge or the lack of clarity about the problem for the overall performance of the firm. Vendors may supply information that clarify the nature of the problem.

Market Uncertainty
Some buying centre members may initially reject the vendor's offerings simply because they do not know whether there exist superior offerings on the market. They may therefore delay the decision-making, particularly if they have substantial authority in the overall decision-making process. Here again the vendor can help speed up the decision-making process if its salespeople can assist in providing information about the types of offerings found on the market and indicate how the vendor's offerings compare with other possible offerings.

Transaction Uncertainty
Transaction uncertainty concerns problems that may arise in getting the product/service from the vendor to the buyer. Some buying centre members may be concerned about delivery and post-delivery problems. This may be particularly true for deliveries to customers in foreign countries where logistical problems can be anticipated.

As much of the deliberations with the buying centres are aimed at addressing these uncertainties, by supplying relevant information at appropriate times and stages in the decision making process, the vendor can facilitate and speed up the decision to be taken, preferably in its favour.

Foreign Market Uncertainties

There are some uncertainties related to international business-to-business marketing. For example, where decision on a vendor's offerings is to be made by buying centre members located in different countries (e.g. selling machines to an international joint venture company) it is important to note that the buying centre members may have different preferences due to the diversity of their backgrounds. The information needs of each of the buying centre members must therefore be carefully studied and catered for.

Furthermore, depending on their specific situations and preferences, the buying centre members may have different priorities. This may be a problem in situations of joint financing. The purchase decision-making may be delayed. A prolonged decision making process can impact on the vendor's marketing efforts negatively, since it will mean that less resources can be devoted to other clients. Figure 8.2 provides a general model of considerations underlying b-t-b decision making process.

Figure 8.2 An Integrated Model for Analyzing Business-to-Business Buying Behaviour

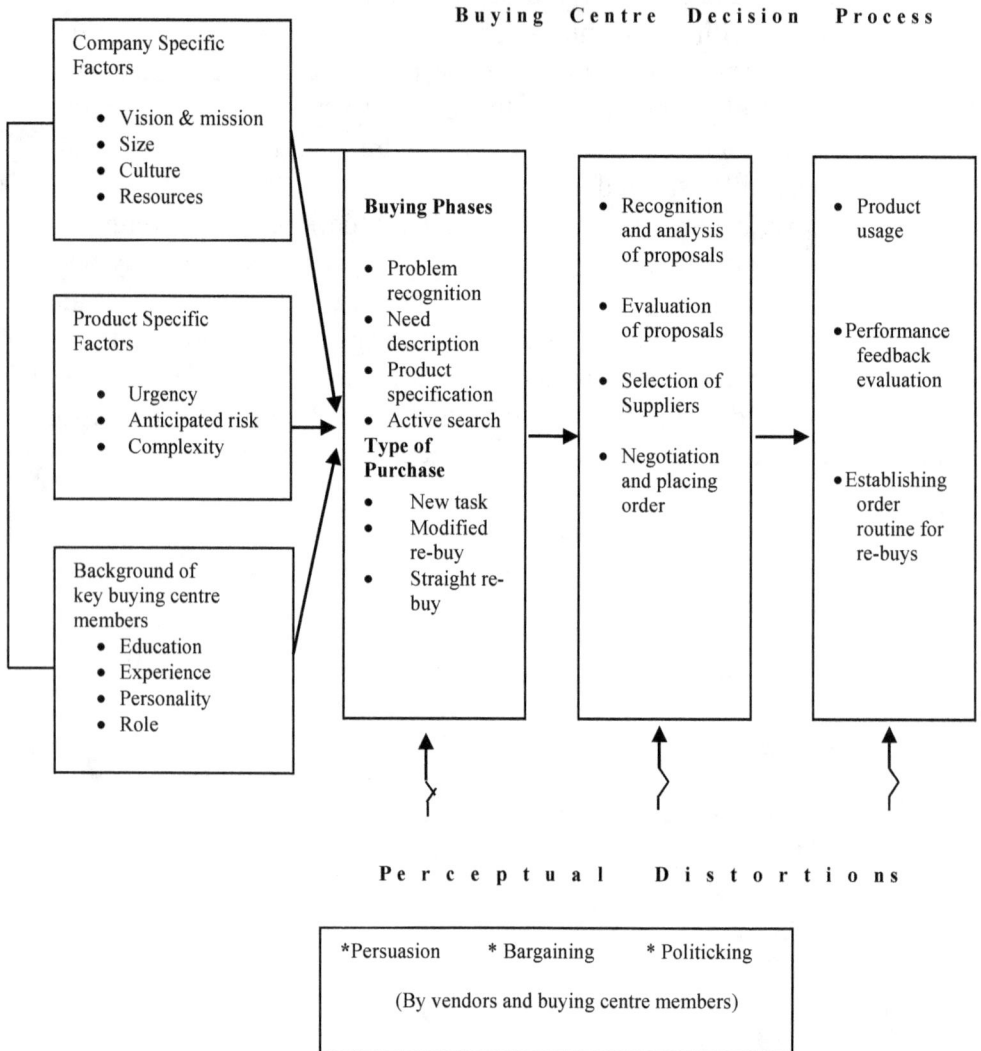

B u y i n g   C e n t r e   D e c i s i o n   P r o c e s s

Company Specific Factors

- Vision & mission
- Size
- Culture
- Resources

Product Specific Factors

- Urgency
- Anticipated risk
- Complexity

Background of key buying centre members

- Education
- Experience
- Personality
- Role

Buying Phases

- Problem recognition
- Need description
- Product specification
- Active search

Type of Purchase

- New task
- Modified re-buy
- Straight re-buy

- Recognition and analysis of proposals
- Evaluation of proposals
- Selection of Suppliers
- Negotiation and placing order

- Product usage
- Performance feedback evaluation
- Establishing order routine for re-buys

P e r c e p t u a l   D i s t o r t i o n s

*Persuasion   * Bargaining   * Politicking

(By vendors and buying centre members)

8.7 Summary

Organizational buyers are assumed to make rational purchase decisions. Many people are usually involved in the decision making process and they play different roles in the process. The process usually starts with problem recognition when the problem faced by the organization is recognized or a need for a new product or service is identified. This is followed by a general description of the nature of products/services/ solution that is required. The general description is then translated into product/service specifications, leading to an initiation of a supplier search process. When appropriate suppliers are identified, some individuals are assigned the task of soliciting proposals from them after which one of the vendors will be selected among them.

Who makes the decision to buy depends in part on the situation. Three types of buying situations have been distinguished: the straight rebuy, the modified rebuy, and the new task. The straight rebuy is the simplest situation: The company reorders a good or service without any modifications. With the modified rebuy, the buyer is seeking to modify product specifications, prices, and so on. The purchaser is interested in negotiation, and several participants may take part in the buying decision. A company faces a new task when it considers buying a product for the first time. The number of participants and the amount of information sought tend to increase with the cost and risks associated with the transaction. This situation represents the best opportunity for the marketer.

References

Bunn, Michele D., (1993) "Taxonomy of Buying Decision Approaches, *Journal of Marketing* Vol 57, 38-56

Choffray, J.J.; Lilien, G.L. (1980) "Industrial market segmentation by the Structure of the purchasing process" *Industrial Marketing Management*, Vol 91 No. 41 pp. 331.342

Mowery, D., Oxley, J.E., and Silverman, B., (1996) "Strategic Alliance and Business-to-business Knowledge Transfer" *Strategic Management Journal* 17 (4): 77-91

Osmonbekov, T., Bello, D. & Gilliland, D. (2002) "Adoption of Electronic Commerce Tools in Business Procurement: Enhanced Buying Center Structure and Processes." *Journal of Business and Industrial Marketing*, 17 (2/3): 151-166.

Robinson, Patrick J., Faris, Charles W., and Wind Yoram (1967) *Industrial Buying and Creative Marketing* (Boston: Allyn and Bacon)

Sheth, J.N. (1973): "A Model of Industrial Buying behaviour." *Journal of Marketing*, Vol 37, No.4, pp. 50-56

Webster Frederick E. Jr. and Wind, Yoram (1972)"A General Model for Understanding Organizational Buying behaviour " *Journal of Marketing*, Vol. 36, No.2 pp.12-19

For Further Readings

Vitale, R., Giglierano, J., Pfoertsch, W. (2010) *Business-to-Business Marketing*, (Boston, Pearson Education Inc)

Fill, Chris and Fill, Karen (2005) *Business-to-Business Marketing* (Essex, Person Eductation Inc)

CHAPTER NINE

Online Advertising Decisions and Strategies[2]

9.1 Introduction

The 21 century has ushered in a radical change in advertising strategies of companies. Companies increasingly see the Internet as an important medium through which advertising messages can be directed towards customers and consumers in both business-to-business and business-to-consumer market segments. The increased adoption of Internet by households during the past two decades has also made significant contribution to this trend. The growing understanding among practitioners is that marketers no longer have the option of treating people like audiences because people no longer have to sit around and respectfully listen to their message. They have choices. With the democratization and socialization of information, people tend to reason in the following manner: "why would I accept a final product that doesn't work for me when I can go elsewhere and help build one? Why would I continue to watch TV commercials when I have TiVo? Why would I stay on your web site if I don't like it? Why would I buy your product when I know there are 10 other better options for less money? Why would I listen to a canned message when I can speak directly with the creator"?[3]

Thus, although the Internet allows companies to create awareness and provide product information that can influence consumer attitudes and behaviour, it has also shifted the power of control over advertising exposure from the advertiser to the potential viewer and therefore complicates advertising strategy formulation as well as the measurement of online advertising effects. In effect, viewers can now select how much commercial content they wish to view.

Despite the remarkable growth in online transactions and advertisement, research into the impact of the Internet on marketing is

---

[2] This chapter builds on Eriksen, Kim and Kuada, John (2009) *Recent Developments in Online Advertising* (International Business Centre, Study Material Series No. 17, Aalborg University) pp. 1- 13

[3] Josh Chambers, Strategy Specialist (http://www.viget.com/engage/relational-marketing-is-the-future/)

still at a nascent stage and strategic guidelines for managers are very limited. Marketers therefore repeatedly expose Internet users to the same techniques found in traditional form of advertising (Campbell and Wright, 2008).

The primary goal of this chapter is to provide an overview of the existing online advertising tools and the theoretical rationale underlying them. It starts with a brief introduction to advertising theories.

9.2 Advertising Theories and Online Advertising

Advertising is described in the marketing literature as any paid form of non-personal presentation and promotion of ideas, goods or services by an identified sponsor. Earlier advertising perspectives have been guided largely by ideas found in the communication and psychological literature. The emphasis has been to understand the stages that customers pass through before making purchase decisions. It has been assumed that the more exposure a potential customer has to a stimulus the more he/she will tend to like it. Subsequent studies have however suggested more nuanced perspectives on how marketers can influence consumer purchase decisions. These studies have shown that there is a strong relationship between consumer involvement and information processing. The understanding is that a highly involved consumer, who has the ability and motivation to process information, will undertake extensive cognitive processing, particularly when the information offered is personally relevant. Personal relevance is therefore an essential characteristic for involvement, and this idea has been commonly used in attitude-based persuasions.

Concepts such as persuasiveness, brand awareness, emotions and attitudes have therefore become prominent in the advertising literature during the past half a century. These ideas have informed several prescriptive models of advertising that are found in marketing textbooks. Notable examples of these models include the popular Attention, Interest, Desire, Action (AIDA) formula and its numerous hierarchy-of-effects derivatives.

A significant objective of advertising is attitude change. A consumer's attitude toward a product refers to his or her beliefs about, feeling toward, and purchase intentions for the product. Beliefs can be both positive (e.g., for McDonald's food: tastes good, is convenient) and negative (is high in fat). In general, it is usually very difficult to change deeply held beliefs. Thus, in most cases, the advertiser may be better off trying to add a belief (e.g., beef is convenient) rather than trying to change one (beef is really not very fatty).

Consumer receptivity to messages aimed at altering their beliefs will tend to vary a great deal depending on the nature of the product. For unimportant products such as soft drinks, research suggests that consumers are often persuaded by having a large number of arguments with little merit presented (e.g., the soda comes in a neat bottle, the bottle contains five per cent more soda than competing ones). In contrast, for high involvement, more important products, consumers tend to scrutinize arguments more closely, and will tend to be persuaded more by high quality arguments.

Building on the theoretical understandings found in the marketing literature, online advertisement may be seen as consisting of any content on a Web site which intends to act as a commercial device to carry a message or attract a user. This may typically take the form of a static image or a text message, but could also be a Real Audio stream, or an animated image.

Marketers perceive advertising as a service. As such, online advertising aims to provide consumers with information and capabilities that soften transactions or enhance brand engagement. The first approach for the companies is to identifying the services and information the consumers requires, and then create the messages and experiences relevant to those needs.

Online advertising has several similarities to traditional advertising since it entails persuasion through communication and both appeal to the cognitive and emotional processes of potential customers. But there are significant differences as well.

In the case of online advertising, personal relevance of messages and nature of interactivity have been shown to strongly affect advertising effectiveness (Fortin and Dholakia, 2005). Interactivity here is defined in terms of the extent to which users can participate in modifying the form and content of a mediated environment in real time. It consists of three factors: 1) speed - the rate at which content can be manipulated 2) range - ability of content to be manipulated 3) mapping - the similarity between the controls and how the content is manipulated. Because of these three dimensions, an online advertisement can have varying levels of interactivity. An advertisement can be slow or fast in its exposure (speed), dynamic or static (range), and intuitive or unintuitive (mapping) in its interaction with the user (Campbell and Wright, 2008).

Online environment has also been found to be richer than traditional advertising channels and therefore have a strong impact on the effect of online advertisements to the extent that it influences consumer attitudes. Due to this richness, it has been argued that simply applying the principle of repetition does not make logical sense. Furthermore, online advertising can be targeted at much smaller segments, and the performance of an ad can be measured with regards to number of clicks, views and purchases. Time spent on a specific page can be recorded and even mouse tracking or a quick pop up upon departure can provide further data to evaluate advertising performance. The focus of online advertising is therefore the single individual behind the screen; each can be identified and targeted with the use of software. An international campaign can still be used, but the simple mass broadcast message is obsolete. The visitor is in focus rather than that of the product and its characteristics.

Online advertising has also been described as being characterized by "herd-behaviour" – i.e. a tendency whereby people's decisions are influenced by the behaviour of others. The manifestation of the "herd behaviour" is seen in the fact that online messages cover the globe in seconds. Therefore a successful site such as facebook.com has millions of users. The question is, however, if the site is successful because it has a product that millions of users want, or if the site is just popular because of herd-behaviour.

The herd behaviour can be compared to *viral marketing*. Stated simply, the argument underlying viral marketing is that if the message is interesting to large numbers of people, it will be shared by a larger number of people. An example can be found at youtube.com, where top lists of different videos can be found. Not only most viewed (which is obvious), but also most recent, - discussed or active. The herd behaviour is illustrated here by the fact that when browsing videos one notices that those videos that appear to be viewed a lot more will continue to attract the attention of new visitors to the sites.

When consumers want to know specifications and details, like engines, trim lines, or safety features, they turn to branded sources. But when it comes to more direct and personal information such as ratings, reliability, and quality, consumers are unlikely to evaluate manufacturers' claims by turning to sources they consider more independent and objective. Depending on the promotional objectives sought by a particular company, different advertising strategies and approaches may be taken. The following are some content strategies commonly used.

- *Information dissemination/persuasion.* Comparative ads attempt to get consumers to believe that the sponsoring product is better. Although these are frequently disliked by Americans, they tend to be among the most effective ads in the U.S. Comparative advertising is illegal in some countries and is considered very inappropriate culturally in some societies, especially in Asia.
- *Fear appeals* try to motivate consumers by telling them the consequences of not using a product. Mouthwash ads, for example, talk about how gingivitis and tooth loss can result from poor oral hygiene. It is important, however, that a specific way to avoid the feared stimulus be suggested directly in the ad. Thus, simply by using the mouthwash advertised, these terrible things can be avoided.
- *Attitude change through the addition of a belief.* This topic was covered under consumer behaviour. As a reminder, it is usually easier to get the consumer to accept a new belief which is not inconsistent with what he or she already believes than it is to change currently held beliefs.
- *Classical conditioning.* A more favourable brand image can often be created among the consumer when an association to a liked object or idea is created. For example, an automobile can be paired with a beautiful woman or a product can be shown in a very upscale setting.
- *Humour appeal.* The use of humour in advertisements is quite common. This method tends not to be particularly useful in persuading the consumer. However, more and more advertisers find themselves using humour in order to compete for the consumer's attention. Often, the humour actually draws attention *away* from the product—people

will remember what was funny in the ad but not the product that was advertised. Thus, for ads to be effective, the product advertised should be an integral part of what is funny.

- *Repetition.* Whatever specific objective is sought, repetition is critical. This is especially the case when the objective is to communicate specific information to the customer. Advertising messages—even simple ones—are often understood by consumers who have little motive to give much attention to advertisements to which they are exposed. Therefore, very little processing of messages is likely to be done at any one time of exposure. Cumulatively, however, a greater effect may result.
- *Celebrity endorsements.* Celebrities are likely to increase the amount of attention given to an advertisement. However, these celebrities may not be consistently persuasive.

9.3 Online Advertising Models and their Rationale

The dominant models of advertising can be classified into the following three categories

1. *On Demand model,* which is based on consumers' abilities to select and choose their content and interactions with brands.
2. *The engagement model,* where visitors are engaged in the product or service.
3. *Advertising as service to consumers*, where the simplicity of a website becomes an advantage.

9.3.1 On Demand Model

Storage, retrieval, and on-demand access have transformed the media business and increased the value of its content. The essential part of this model is the approach to the consumer as satisfied participant. The era of consumers reading, watching, or listening on the media schedules seems almost disappearing. Even network television, which built its business on aggregating viewers at specific times, is experimenting with On Demand models. Episodes of some programmes, even wildly popular ones, are sold on Apple's iTunes, or made available from their own online distribution systems like CBS' Innertube, or through the shows' own websites. Through these websites it is possible to watch news 24 hours a day. In fact, many media have enjoyed an unforeseen benefit from the on-demand trend: their archives have become hot properties because consumers seek access to materials from hours, days, weeks, or years ago.

Broadly adopted information search tools are important developments supporting the On Demand model. Before search engines and good websites, consumers were forced to seek brand information and knowledge from the manufacturers, retailers, and distributors. Capable search and websites optimised for search engines changed that situation. Today consumers have access to product information 24/7.

Another important aspect of the On Demand model is satisfied personalisation. Consumers want to leverage and connect the knowledge power of brands by customising content to their personal interests, needs, and tastes. This takes the form of managing preferences: "I want to see the weather in the 9500 and 9800 zip codes on my home page," "Update me only when there's new information about a certain Brand X". Consumers like choices, but with choice comes responsibility. If they have too many choices, they will get confused, irritable or immobilised and this will be counter productive.

To address the irritations of "choice overload", new and powerful options have now been developed by software engineers to accept or reject brand messages. For example, it is possible for most Internet users today to avoid pop-ups and other unwanted advertising mails only by adding pop-ups killers. It is therefore necessary for brand marketers today to take these new tools into consideration in order to stimulate the demand for their products and services. Due to the many media types and the consumers' behaviour they become uniquely individual and their choices also become individual choices and therefore cause many complications for the advertiser. These situations differentiate the traditional view of segmentation and signify that new types of thinking are needed to exploit the advertising opportunities.

9.3.2 Engagement Model

The Engagement model is based upon two key ideas:

1. High relevance of brands to consumers
2. The development of an emotional connection between consumers and brands.

161

Because engagement is based on emotions and relationships between customers and companies, it is also described by such concepts as bonding, shared meaning, and identification, concepts that emphasize the connectivity of customers to brands of advertised products.

Customer connectivity and engagement strategies are based on multiple sources of consumer data. For example, standard learning and opinion polls (familiar to 30-second TV spots) or online banners such as brand awareness and purchase intention are the essential foundation in understanding what customers think of. They are used to involve, inform, entertain, and in a longer term, to co-evolve consumers through the creation and ongoing development of brand meaning.

Some online websites have pop-up help windows which are meant to be services to customers. Pop-ups appear when a shopper (customer) has performed a certain amount of searches in a short period of time. The reason for having such items may be that customers are having difficulties finding items that they are interested in or just not sure what they want. Such services can be more specific, based on previous behaviour on the specific site.

9.3.2 Advertising as a Service

Advertising as a service is perhaps the most personal of the three models. Marketers need to make sure they deliver a helpful service at the appropriate times and avoid the trap of substituting technology for consumer insight and connection.

Sites must not be too difficult to navigate through. The average consumer demands simplicity and value of the individual sites. In the consumer-driven approach, consumer wants are the drivers of all strategic marketing decisions. No strategy is pursued until it passes the test of consumer research. Every aspect of a market offering, including the nature of the product itself, is driven by the needs of potential consumers. This implies that the best test of quality of an online advertisement should be what information services the consumer gains from the ad.

9.4 Marketing and Online Advertising Tools

Online advertising has been applied aggressively in recent years to support online marketing strategies. We present some of the main tools used in this section of the chapter. They include forums, chats, viral marketing processes, email marketing, banner ads, pop-ups and searches.

9.4.1 Forums/Chat and Product Endorsements

Chat and forums are one of the more widely used ways of engaging visitors, by allowing them chat options. Through both support chat and user chat, visitors have options of committing themselves to a site and/or brand. Chatting has evolved into one of the most used functions of the Internet. Programmes such as MSN Messenger, Yahoo Messenger and the now outdated ICQ (I seek you) are among the most downloaded and used programmes online[4]. Forums are found on many different pages, mostly used to link up people with a specific issue. Today forums can also be found on sites discussing news or politics.

Chat is about dialogue, but interactions between people are now turning towards blogging. Posting thoughts and actions online is quickly becoming an everyday activity for many people. People in many different positions are posting thoughts about politics, sports, clothes etc. Successful blogs can have millions of viewers. An example from Sweden is (http://www.blondinbella.se/) where a teenager interested in politics started blogging about her involvement in youth politics, but the blog turned at some point into a description about her life in general, makeup, clothes and cafés, suddenly she became a trendsetter for teenagers, and companies have since been paying her to write about their products. Discussions about the right to blog and be paid for it without disclosing it to the readers have however stirred some debate.[5]

---

[4]There are no reliable sources as most downloads are only monitored by the producers. Estimates on number of users differ greatly.
[5]See for instance http://jilltxt.net/?p=2257

9.4.2 Viral marketing

As noted earlier, viral marketing is word of mouth translated into Internet marketing, and can be seen as the herd-behaviour in social relations. Many people have a tradition for passing funny emails on, or having a specific Friday ritual of wishing good weekend with a joke. This social relational phenomenon has now become part of a marketing tool, whereby ambassadors of products create advertising by highlighting their experiences with products or service. In this way, viral marketing has become cheaper than normal advertising option since the advertiser, in theory, only has to post the advertisement at one place, and let it spread from there. Furthermore viral marketing is often not even perceived as commercial advertising, as the person behind the message often is a friend or co-worker. Viral marketing often has the possibility to reach consumers that a company normally would not reach with any advertising option. Many companies today are very much aware of viral marketing, and typically have their advertising material available online and allow for such materials to be sent to friends.

9.4.3 Email marketing

Email marketing is often referred to as a spam. It is used where companies do not care who they target and just mass distribute their messages. But contrary to popular belief, email marketing is not entirely a waste. Many companies have newsletters, and many sites provide the option of making a specific search string possible to be received daily or weekly. For example, jobsites use this to tell job seekers about new entries to their database.

The task is to make the mail relevant and at the right time. A thorough programme of triggered messages (sent individually based on Web site behaviour) can provide tremendous information about a subscriber while simultaneously delivering hyper-relevant and timely information. This means that companies contemplating the use of email marketing must analyse visitors to web sites in order to know when to send a specific message to a particular visitor.

9.4.4 Banner Ads

One of the most widely used forms of advertising online is that of the banner ad. The ad is placed on a website, and usually highlights itself with different colours, size and motion. It can be a punch line, a question or even a video. It has evolved with the discovery of newer tools and programmes. In the beginning the banner was a non-moving square with a text and/or picture, but today it is often a video that starts with a mouse over. Therefore the banner ad can be compared to an outdoor communication form that developed with the Internet.

Several researchers have shown that banner ads also have an impact on consumers' attitude toward a brand independent of click-through rate. It was shown that banner ads have longer-term effects that help build brand equity and can successfully raise brand awareness, preference, and consumer purchase intentions.

The ROI for banners are measured in two ways, firstly the brand awareness, where the remembrance of the message or brand name is important. Secondly by a rate of interaction - the *click through rate* (CTR) – the higher the number of people who click on the banner, the higher the value the advertiser has been given. It has been found that repetition reduces CTR.

Banner ad has been studied since the beginning of the commercialised Internet. Many different angles of discussions and conclusions have been drawn, and there are several counter perceptions. The form of the banner, the size, placement on the page, colour and sound etc. are all factors to be considered in order to emphasise messages.

Several studies also looked into improving Internet banner advertising effectiveness by optimizing the placement of ads (Cho, *et al.*, 2001; Dou, *et al.*, 2001; Moore, *et al.*, 2005). By using target market analysis, Sherman and Deighton (2001) have found that the average cost per response can be reduced nine-fold when advertising on Web sites because visitors are disproportionately likely to respond to banner advertising. Likewise, Manchanda *et al.* (1999) have shown that banner ads have an impact on Internet purchasing and that click-through rates are a poor indicator of the effect of banner ad exposure on sales.

Studies also show that the message on the banner can have an impact. Mentioning of price, gift, or free offers actually reduce CTR, while banners with neither price nor promotional offers have bigger influence on CTR and brand remembrance.

This suggests that advertising via banners is more than just having the brand name, or making a good promotional offer. It is necessary to target the specific consumer via the correct host website, and it also needs to be with the correct message. This is not different from that of offline marketing, but the Internet has created an option that makes customer targeting simpler than otherwise. It is possible to track where the visitor is from via the ISP (Internet service provider), what search words were used to visit a particular website (what website did the visitor leave to visit the current) and determine whether the visitor is a first timer on the focal site, or a frequent visitor.

CTR is slowly declining, and advertising can now be bought with PPC (pay-per click). Google offers a large range of advertising options that is based on clicks rather than views. There is however the problem of fraud in relation to PPC – some people's intention may simply be to make the advertiser pay for his/her clicks.

9.4.5 Pop-ups

The pop-up is defined by new "opens" on top of the one the visitor is currently visiting. There are several variations of the pop-up:

- The pop-under, opening a website under the one currently being visited.
- The pop-in; where something is blurred or covered at the visited website in order to advertise for something.

Pop-ups can be designed to appear when a website is loading, after a period of time is spent on a website, or upon leaving the site/closing the window. Pop-ups can appear as small windows covering a portion of the host website, it can therefore be less intrusive.

The pop-up has been perceived as very annoying, and has often been compared to that of advertising breaks on TV. Several pop-up killers[6] have been introduced online. Several other bigger software producers have included pop-up killer software in their programmes, and major advertisers have disregarded the option of pop-up advertising.

9.5 Search Advertising and Web Site Design

Google has developed the option of search advertising. The concept is that any given word typed into a search engine, can be bought. This way, the results shown is on the one hand the result of the search concept, but a new list of advertising is available (typically in a different list than that of the search results). Here the buyer of the word gets advertising space. The more popular the word is, the more expensive it is to buy.

But search advertising can be other things. Shopping comparison sites are gaining popularity, and thus it will be important for a company to be represented on the most important sites. Ebay is not only private sellers, but a large number of professional sellers, usually with brand new products are present, and are competing for attention with the private sellers.

Issues that must be taken into account in web site design include the following:

- *Speed vs. aesthetics*: As we saw, some of the fancier sites have serious problems functioning practically. Consumers may be impressed by a fancy site, or may lack confidence in a company that offers a simple one. Yet, fancier sites with extensive graphics take time to download—particularly for users dialing in with a modem as opposed to being "hard" wired—and may result in site crashes.
- *Keeping users on the site:* A large number of "baskets" are abandoned online as consumers fail to complete the "check-out" process for the products they have selected. One problem here is that many consumers are drawn away from a site and then are unlikely to come back. A large number of links may be desirable to consumers, but they tend to draw people away. Taking banner advertisers on your site from other sites may be profitable, but it may result in loss of customers.

---

[6] A small programme that terminates the pop-up before it opens

- *Information collection*: An increasing number of consumers resist collection of information about them, and a number of consumers have set up their browsers to disallow "cookies," files that contain information about their computers and shopping habits.
- *Site content.*The content of a site should generally be based on the purposes of operating a site. The site should generally provide some evidence for this position. For example, if the site claims a large selection, the vast choices offered should be evident. Sites that claim convenience should make this evident. A main purpose of the Internet is to make information readily available, and the site should be designed so that finding the needed information among all the content of the site is as easy as possible. Since it is easy for consumers to move to other sites, the site should be made interesting. To provide the information and options desired by customers, two-way interaction capabilities are essential.

9.6 Summary

The web is now so large that getting traffic to any one site can be difficult. One method is search engine optimization, a topic that will be covered below. Other methods include "viral" campaigns wherein current users are used to spread the word about a site, company, or service. For example, Google offers a free e-mail account with a full gigabyte of storage. This is available only by invitation from others who have such e-mail accounts. Amazon.com at one point invited people, when they had completed a purchase, to automatically e-mail friends whose e-mail addresses they provided with a message about what they had just bought. If the friend bought any of the same items, both the original customer and the friend would get a discount.

References

Brumer G.C., and Kumar A (2000) "Web commercials and advertising hierarchy of effects" *Journal of Advertising Research* Vol.35, 35-42

Campbell, Damon E. and Wright, Ryan T. (2008) "Shut-Up I Don't Care: Understanding the Role of Relevance and Interactivity on Customer Attitudes toward Repetitive Online Advertising" *Journal of Electronic Commerce Research* Vol. 9, Iss. 1; pp: 62-76

Cho, Chang-Hoan, Jung-Gyo Lee, and Marye Tharp (2001), "Different Forced-Exposure Levels to Banner Advertisements," *Journal of Advertising Research,* Vol. 41 No. 4 pp: 45-56.

Dholakia, N., and Soltysinski, (2001) "Coveted or overlooked? The psychology of bidding for comparable listings in digital auctions" *Marketing Letters* Vol.12 pp: 223-235

Dou, Wenyu, Linn, Randy and Yang, Sixian (2001), "How Smart Are Smart Banners: A Scoreboard and Analysis", *Journal of Advertising Research*, Vol. 41, No.4, pp: 31-44

Fortin, David R. and Dholakia, Ruby Roy (2005), "Interactivity and Vividness Effects on Social Presence and Involvement with a web-based Advertisement," *Journal of Business Research*, Vol.58, No.3 pp: 387-396.

Manchanda, Puneet Ansari, Asim and Gupta, Sunil (1999) "The "Shopping Basket": A Model for Multicategory Purchase Incidence Decisions" *Marketing Science* Vol. 18, No. 2 pp. 95-114

Moore, Robert, Stammerjohan, C., and Coulter, R (2005). "The Effects of Ad-Web Site Congruity and Execution Cues on Attention and Attitudes," *Journal of Advertising,* Vol.34 No. 2 pp: 77-90.

Schadler, T. & Golvin, C.S. (2006) The state of consumers and technology: Benchmark Forrester Research. July 17 [WWW document]. URL http://www.forrester.com (accessed on 21 January 2009).

Sherman, Lee and John Deighton (2001), "Banner Advertising: Measuring Effectiveness and Optimizing Placement," *Journal of Interactive Marketing* Vol. 15 No.2 pp: 60-64

For Further Readings

Goldsmith, R., (2002) "Explaining and Predicting Consumer Intention to Purchase Over the Internet: An Exploratory Study", *Journal of Marketing*, Vol.66 pp: 22-28

Mehta, Abhilasha. (2000) "Advertising attitudes and advertising effectiveness" *Journal of Advertising Research*, Vol. 40 No.3 pp:67-71

CHAPTER TEN

Assessment of Export Opportunities

10.1 Introduction

Chapter four provides a general framework for analysing market opportunities. The present chapter builds on the discussion and focuses attention on how international companies can identify export opportunities. In specific terms, it takes a look at how information is assembled, analysed and communicated to managers to support executive decisions. It takes the reader through some of the conventional approaches to market selection and monitoring aimed at identifying trends and possible shifts within the potential and current market environments of international companies. It also discusses such concepts as market concentration and market risk analysis while drawing readers' attention to problems of conducting international market research in general.

The chapter begins by describing seven useful steps that decision makers may take in the process of planning their marketing strategies. It then continues with a discussion of a systematic approach to export market opportunity identification. This includes a description of a model for screening prospective markets and selecting a few that meet the strategic objectives of a company. The chapter then continues with a discussion of the differences between market concentration and market spreading strategies. It also has a short section on marketing risk analysis.

10.2 Steps in International Marketing Strategy Development

The following steps can guide most international marketing strategy formulation. Although the steps are presented here sequentially, in practice, they function iteratively, with planners reverting to earlier steps when considered necessary for improvement of their work process.

1. Set marketing objectives for the product/service in focus.
2. Conduct product analysis.
3. Perform market segmentation analysis,
4. Evaluate segments in terms of the company's marketing objectives.

171

5. Assess the marketing requirements for serving the various segments.
6. Rank the strategy options in terms of goal attainment index.
7. Suggest the appropriate strategy and develop an implementation plan.

10.2 1 Specifying Marketing Objectives

Marketing executives must specify the objectives that should guide the analysis – i.e. help evaluate (a) the attractiveness of the market, and (b) the alternative strategies that the analyst may want to consider. Most marketing textbooks list the following five objectives as among the key objectives that a company may have in a given market.

1. Profit level that the company considers to be acceptable when it enters a given market. Management must also specify the number of years (months) after which their investments in the market should start to yield profit.
2. Sales growth, indicating how rapidly the company would want its sales volume to increase in the target market (Note that increase in sales volume may not necessarily produce profit).
3. Market share, indicating what proportion of the total market the company would want to take during a given period of time.
4. Degree of risk, indicating the degree of change in market trends that the company is willing to accept. That is, to what extent should demand fall before the company withdraws its investments in that market?
5. Resource commitment, indicating the amount of resources (money, time and staff involvement) that the company is willing to devote to the market in question.

It is possible that your contact person cannot provide you with full answers to all these points. You must base your analysis on those dimensions that management has specified.

10.2. 2 Conduct a Product Analysis

This analysis provides you an insight into the company's product attributes and its relative strengths/weaknesses compared to competitors' products. It also guides you in defining any unique characteristics you may emphasise in communicating the values and

172

benefits offered by the product to potential customers. Key questions to guide this analysis include the following:

1. What are the company's key products that it expects to sell in the target markets?
2. What customer values/benefits do they offer?
3. What attributes distinguish them from similar products offered by competitors?
4. Do the products benefit from any positive country of origin effect or brand image?
5. Is the company engaged in continuous research and development aimed at re-designing or upgrading the products?

Products are usually classified in terms of *core product attributes, tangible/enhanced product attributes* and *augmented product attributes*. This classification can serve as a useful starting point. But it is important to discuss with the executives as to whether other industry-specific classifications can be applied in the specific analysis. It is also important to have some idea of the degree of geographical spread that the company wishes to achieve. This dimension addresses the issue as to whether the product is international, or global. International products are sold in few selected countries or regional markets such as the EU. Global products are sold in the world's major markets and several other markets. Such products also have the potential of fulfilling needs of consumers throughout the world. Finally, it is important to know whether the product appeals to the high, medium or low end of the market.

10.2. 3 Perform Market Segmentation Analysis

This step starts with an identification of the relevant segmentation criteria for the company's products and the market in question. Consult any marketing textbook for inspiration. Your contact person may help you with this and even indicate whether the company was interested in some specific segments. In case of b-t-b marketing, segmentation analysis provides the analyst with an opportunity to assess the attractiveness of each segment separately.

Having identified the relevant segments, each of them must be analysed using the following segment attractiveness index:

1. Stage of segment maturity in the target country
2. Current segment size
3. Key customers' marketing requirements with respect to the following:
   - Product – quality and design
   - Price
   - Service requirements
   - Requirements relating to physical and work environment specifications
   - Delivery requirements
   - Conditions of payment
   - Other transactional cost concerns specified by your company
4. Prospects of segment profitability
5. Degree of competition within the market segment (i.e. how much of the market segment have competitors already served?)

10.2.4 Evaluate Segments in Terms of the Company's Marketing Objectives

This requires a check of the extent to which each of the identified segments can fulfil the company's marketing objectives that have been specified in step one. The analyst can also conduct scenario analysis of the attractive segments. This requires an estimation of the probability that there would be changes within the economic environment of the country and these changes would affect the sizes of the segments and their relative attractiveness (positively or negatively). Information about possible changes in market trend may be obtained from government macroeconomic analysis or analysis undertaken by international economic institutions such as the World Bank/IMF and the OECD. The analyst may also conduct interviews with leading experts in the country for their opinion.

The information may be used to produce three kinds of probability estimate:

(a) An optimistic estimate – i.e. the probability that changes in the economy would raise the size of the market segments and/or improve their profitability by 5-10%.

174

(b) A Normal estimate– i.e. the probability that your estimates are correct.

(c) A pessimistic estimate–i.e. the probability that changes in the economy would lower the size of the market segments and/or reduces their profitability by 5-10%.

10.2.5 Assess the Marketing Requirements for Serving the Various Segments

Under this step, the analyst is required to select the market segments that the analyses have shown to be attractive during the specified time frame (e.g. three years). It will also require the analyst to check for inter-segment similarities and differences in marketing requirements. Determine which segments could be served with minimum efforts/resources.

Some of the key questions to be addressed in the analysis of the marketing requirements of the various market segments are:

1. Is product adaptation necessary to serve this segment? Product adaptation may be necessary for any of the following reasons:
   - Legal requirements
   - Technical requirements
   - Cultural requirements
2. Do customers in the market expect credit? For how long?
3. Do customers expect after sales service? Can such services be provided online? Are there qualified local technicians to be hired for such services?
4. At what prices are similar products sold in the selected market segments?
5. Do customers expect discounts?
6. How stable is the local currency and to what extent do currency exchange fluctuations affect prices?
7. Are there tariff constraints to be taken into account?

10.2.6 Rank the Strategy Options in Terms of Goal Attainment Index

There are four strategic options to consider.

(a) A product specialisation strategy, whereby you advise the company to serve all the segments with the same product.

(b) Segment specialisation strategy, whereby you advise the company to serve a single segment but sell all its product lines and varieties to that segment.

(c) A selective strategy, whereby the company sells specific products to specific segments but limits itself to just a few segments

(d) Single product-segment strategy, whereby you advise the company to sell only one of its products to only one specific segment during the period under consideration.

The choice of strategy should depend on company's marketing or business objectives.

10.2.7 Suggest the Appropriate Strategy and Develop an Implementation Plan

The marketing literature identifies four key determinants of entry mode. These are:

1. Industry-specific determinants, i.e. what is the prevalent approach used in the industry and therefore define customers' minimum expectation.

2. Company-specific determinants, i.e. approach the company is capable of adopting based on its degree of internationalisation, marketing objectives and resource availability.

3. Target market determinants, i.e. distribution policies and regulations in the target country, which the company has to abide by.

4. Home country determinants, i.e. policies and regulations in the company's home country that may influence entry mode decisions.

Marketing strategy should have the following three elements:

1. *Promises*: These include what the company should promise prospective customers in its marketing package. They relate to product

176

features (possible collaboration in the product design in the case of technology), prices, payment conditions, delivery plans, service commitments etc. Promises should meet or even surpass the marketing requirements that your analysis has revealed.

2. *Processes:* This covers plans for how to communicate these values to prospective customers, how to canvas for orders and how to organise the marketing activities. (This is part of the communication parameters in the marketing mix strategy).

3. *Providers*: This covers the organisation of the marketing process. That is who should do what in the value creation and delivery process, at what stages and at what cost.

10.3   Opportunistic and Systematic Approaches to Market Selection

Bradly (2005) distinguishes between two generic approaches to market selection. The first is *opportunistic identification* of markets and the second is a *systematic selection* procedure. The term opportunistic identification covers situations where a given external stimulus or a combination of stimuli brings a foreign market opportunity to the attention of the company. These stimuli may include the company's receipt of unsolicited order or enquiry about its products. This may happen when a third party draws a potential customer's attention to the existence of the company's product or when information about the product reaches the potential customer through the media. Alternatively, opportunistic market identification may occur when any of the company's managers visits another country for non-business reasons and becomes aware of business opportunities there. This event is termed *casual discovery of market potential*. Lastly, opportunities may be discovered through participation in trade missions, exhibitions and fairs.

Using the term "opportunistic" to describe the identification of market opportunities through these means may convey the notion of chance. For some companies in some countries and in some situations, this may be an appropriate description. For companies in other countries, the approach may represent deliberate market search strategies. Asian managers are reputed for positioning themselves strategically in networks of relationships that provide them access to vital market information, particularly in areas of business-to-business marketing. They also make deliberate efforts to visit key distributors of competitive products when they are on holidays in new countries. Thus the separation between work and holidays is not as sharp in these societies as in the West. Moreover, participation in trade missions and similar arrangements may constitute the only deliberate market search efforts made by companies in some countries (See Kuada and Sørensen, 2000).

Systematic approach entails formal processes of data collection and analysis. As hinted earlier, International Business managers are required to continuously assess the world market in order to determine which new markets to enter and which ones to vacate. They are also expected to acquire sufficient market knowledge to take prudent strategic decisions that sustain their competitive positions in their current markets. It has been further argued that the nature and location of selected markets affect a company's ability to co-ordinate its foreign operations and improve its global competitive position.

The available literature suggests two alternative approaches to systematic market selection: the *expansive* approach and the *screening* approach (Albaum *et al.,* 2005). Companies adopting the expansive approach move gradually and incrementally to the international market starting from markets that are geographically and culturally similar to the domestic market. Companies adopting the screening approach do the reverse. The two dominant approaches are discussed below.

10.3.1 The Expansive Approach

As discussed in chapter one, the view that exporting begins with psychologically and culturally close markets and extends sequentially to more distant countries has won a general acceptance in the literature, drawing its validation from some published empirical evidence. The general view is that similarities reduce managers' perceived risk in entering the market and for that matter, the amount of information required for them to make a final decision.

Geographic proximity of the foreign market has been noted to be positively correlated to market similarity since it increases the probability of the two countries sharing cultural values and approaches to business. With a lower cultural distance, the exporting company can more confidently transfer familiar marketing services and methods to the new markets. Marketing personnel can also operate in the new country with less difficulty. The net result is that the overall costs of operating in similar markets are lower than in unfamiliar markets. Small and medium-sized enterprises have therefore been noted to show high preference for geographically close and culturally similar markets, particularly during the initial stages of their internationalisation process.

There is also an observed tendency of companies with established positions in a particular market showing reluctance to move into new, unfamiliar markets even if there are opportunities for them to expand their operations in these markets.

Available empirical evidence indicates that many companies initiate their entry into the export business by fulfilling unsolicited orders from importers hitherto unknown to them (Cavusgil and Nevin, 1981). If the importer proves reliable and places frequent orders, he becomes a key customer and a relationship develops between them. Thus, by agreeing to fill orders placed by the importer/customer, the exporting company indirectly makes a market choice. The relationship may prove enduring or may collapse subject to the turn of events and the degree of trust and mutual benefits it provides the parties. The exporter may opt out of markets where his relationship with original importers could not be sustained or may find substitute channel members in order to maintain his presence in the market if such arrangements prove feasible.

10.3.2 The Screening Approach to Market Selection

The screening approach involves a systematic filtering of the global market using a set of criteria and arriving at a market considered most suitable for the company. Once a country has been identified as a suitable export market, the selection task is focused on analysis of the different relevant market segments in the country and a choice of one or several segments that are most likely to help the company fulfil its export objectives. The aim here is to identify which market offers the greatest marketing opportunity. This involves gathering information about a large number of markets and screening them on the basis of pre-determined criteria. Figure 10.1 provides an illustration of a typical screening model. Each stage of the screening process requires a decision on which variables management considers to be important in conducting a strategically appropriate filter of the countries under consideration. Box10.1 provides samples of variables that may be considered in the screening process.

Some of these variables are easy to evaluate. For example, the macro-economic indicators are considered easiest to evaluate at initial screening stages while the legal as well as social and cultural indicators are more difficult to assess and compare across countries. In spite of the subjective elements that their analyses may contain, the contribution of all the indicators to an overall assessment of a foreign market cannot be underestimated.

Country screening is particularly important if potential customers cannot be easily identified and reliable channel members have not been found to guide the company in its choice of market. The elaborate analysis suggested in the screening model can then serve to reduce the degree of uncertainty that will naturally surround management's decision regarding which market to enter. Critics argue, however, that by defining a market as an entire country, the decision maker's attention is focused initially on macro-economic and non-economic variables and con-siderations, e.g. balance of payment figures, rather than individual custo-mers' needs and payment capabilities. The possibility that a number of customers could have other means of financing their purchases outside the apparent restrictions that the macro-economic indicators suggest is lost to the decision-maker, since these customers are invariably screened out during the first filter and never come up for specific assessment. The screening approach can therefore present a distorted picture of the true market potential of a company's product. This criticism is particularly relevant in cases of business-to-business market potential assessments where sales to each single customer are important to the focal company due to the sizes of these purchases.

There are other situations in which the market search effort may not proceed as described in the screening model. One such situation is where the prospective exporter produces goods and/or services earmarked for few users in a few markets/countries. Sales of specialized equipment for space programme are an evident example. Specialized consultancy services for major projects are another example. In such situations potential customers can be readily identified and contacts made directly without any elaborate search or macroeconomic analysis.

Fig 10.1   Steps in Market Screening Process

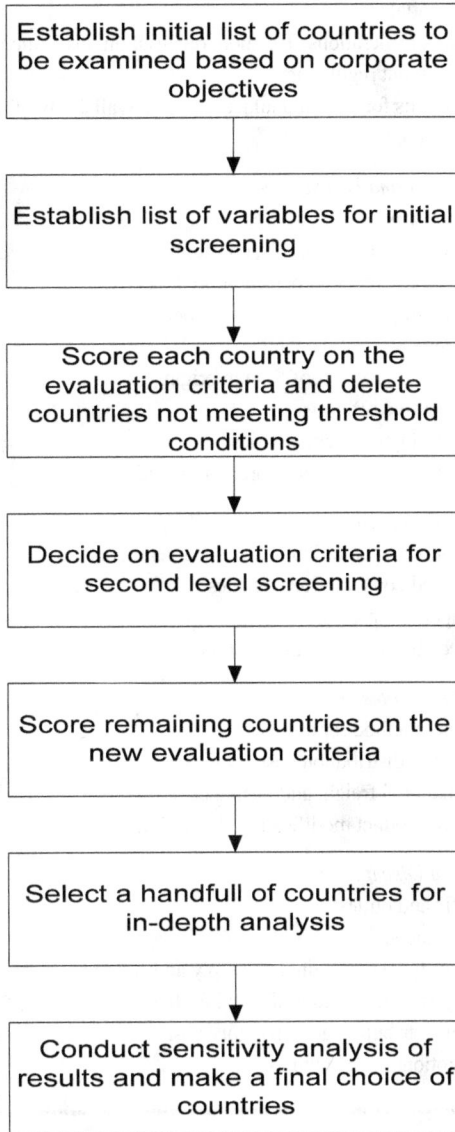

```
┌─────────────────────────────────────┐
│ Establish initial list of countries to│
│ be examined based on corporate       │
│             objectives               │
└─────────────────────────────────────┘
                  │
                  ▼
┌─────────────────────────────────────┐
│ Establish list of variables for initial│
│             screening                │
└─────────────────────────────────────┘
                  │
                  ▼
┌─────────────────────────────────────┐
│     Score each country on the        │
│   evaluation criteria and delete     │
│ countries not meeting threshold      │
│           conditions                 │
└─────────────────────────────────────┘
                  │
                  ▼
┌─────────────────────────────────────┐
│  Decide on evaluation criteria for   │
│       second level screening         │
└─────────────────────────────────────┘
                  │
                  ▼
┌─────────────────────────────────────┐
│  Score remaining countries on the    │
│       new evaluation criteria        │
└─────────────────────────────────────┘
                  │
                  ▼
┌─────────────────────────────────────┐
│  Select a handfull of countries for  │
│          in-depth analysis           │
└─────────────────────────────────────┘
                  │
                  ▼
┌─────────────────────────────────────┐
│   Conduct sensitivity analysis of    │
│ results and make a final choice of   │
│            countries                 │
└─────────────────────────────────────┘
```

Box 10-1
List of Issues Included in In-Depth Analysis of Specific Country
Markets

- *Market Access*
    - Limitations on trade: Tariff levels, quotas etc.
    - Documentation and import regulations
    - Local standards, practices and non-tariff barriers
    - Preferential treaties
    - Legal considerations: Taxation, repatriation, investment, employment regulations
    - Conditions for local manufacture – e.g. availability of qualified labour force

- *Product Potential and Distribution*
    - Customer needs and desires
    - Local production, imports, consumption
    - Exposure to and acceptance of products
    - Availability of complementary products
    - Key indicators of demand
    - Attitude to products of foreign origin
    - Competitive offerings
    - Availability of intermediaries
    - Regional and local transportation facilities

- *Sales Volume Forecasting*
    - Size and concentration of customer segments
    - Projected consumption statistics
    - Competitive pressures
    - Expectations of local distributors/agents

- *Landed Cost Estimates*
    - Costing method for export
    - Domestic distribution cost
    - International freight and insurance
    - Cost of product modification (if required)

- *Cost of internal Distribution*
    - Tariffs and duties
    - Value added tax
    - Cost of local packaging, assembly and storage
    - Margins/Commissions allowed for the trade
    - Local distribution and inventory costs
    - Promotional expenditures

182

10.4   Market Spreading and Market Concentration

Distinction is usually drawn in the export marketing literature between *market concentration* and *market spreading* as strategic options. Market concentration strategy implies that the exporting company focuses on a small number of key markets and develops strong position in them before venturing into new markets. The advantage of this approach is that the amount of resources spent in controlling and co-ordinating international transactions (relative to volume of exports) is lower. But in situations where the markets are selected on the basis of initial responses to customers' orders, it is doubtful if these markets would provide the company with the best export opportunities. If a company decides not to enter new markets despite unfavourable performance in the existing markets, this may reflect management's aversion to risk or complacency at lower performance levels.

Companies appear, however, to show some reluctance in conducting active searches for new markets even for products with market spread potentials. Once a company has found a fairly reliable distributor in its initial export market it expects the distributor to undertake subsequent market expansion on its behalf. In situations where the initial importer/distributor proves unreliable, the company's continued presence and subsequent penetration into that market would depend on its ability to disengage its current relationship and find new importers/distributors for its products or adopt measures that improve its ability to supervise the marketing process. Where no enforceable contractual relationships exist between the company and its current distributor, the cost of switching to another distributor is mainly the opportunity cost of finding a new one. Where the supplier is attractive and the channel system is highly competitive, finding a new importer/distributor would not pose a major problem. But if the reverse is true, switching to a new channel member becomes a less attractive option.

Empirical studies have shown that market *concentrators* tend, in general, to be smaller companies, exhibiting a greater interest in export profitability but, simultaneously, being less concerned with export sales objectives. They also appear to place greater emphasis in their export marketing strategy on regular visits to overseas markets.

10.5 Market Risk Analysis

Since marketing managers are charged with allocating resources in such a way as to ensure the attainment of a company's business objectives, there are always risks associated with their decisions. We have drawn attention to how changes within and outside the company can induce risks. Risks, as we said earlier, are the potential variances between investments and outcomes and the probabilities that these will occur. Within the context of export marketing it makes sense to argue that the selection of target markets is the first critical decision affecting the riskiness of a company's international marketing strategy.

The choice of market reflects management's judgement of the degree and type of risk the company is prepared to accept. A distinction can be drawn between macroenvironment-induced risks and risks related to specific management decisions. Macro level risks are generally subsumed under the concept of political risks. This term covers all sorts of political initiatives that reduce foreign business performance in a given country. In some extreme cases global companies may run the risks of losing control of the management of their foreign subsidiaries or ownership of their assets abroad. Some of the risks may be more tolerable. For example, customs delays or problems of getting visas for expatriates (i.e. political harassment) are easier to deal with. Such other problems as asset ownership losses can have serious negative consequences on the overall performance of some companies.

Loss of asset ownership can happen in one of three ways: confiscation, expropriation, or nationalisation. Confiscation occurs when government decides to take over control of the company's assets in the country without compensation. Expropriation differs from confiscation only in the sense that some compensation is offered for the take-over. Confiscation is usually provided with political legitimacy where it involves companies engaged in exploiting the non-renewable natural resources of a country, e.g. within the mining industry. Nationalisation may affect both domestic and foreign businesses and governments may be prepared to give full compensation for the assets that have been nationalised.

There are also risks associated with specific marketing decisions. Said differently, a company's capacity to produce, promote, and distribute its products is built with marketing investments and their associated risks. Cook and Page (1987) draw a useful distinction between *primary-demand risks* and *market-share risks.* The understanding they put forward is that the size of a market that a company targets influences the amount of marketing resources that management is likely to assign to capturing it – i.e. a large market is inherently riskier than a smaller one. Similarly, the size of market segment that a company's product portfolio addresses, and the share of the market segments in the total market demand for the company's product will also influence marketing budgets assigned to the segment and therefore affect the overall marketing risk. In other words, if the company seeks to serve a small market (or market segment) with stable demand, the risk of the related marketing strategy should be considered low.

Market-share risk arises from building, harvesting, and balancing decisions. These decisions are a product of management's search for differential advantage, the firm's strategic objectives, and budget allocations among the factors of marketing. The higher the probability of variations in cost and revenue estimates associated with these strategic decisions the higher the risks of the marketing investments. Anticipated deviations reflect management uncertainty with respect to both consumer response (variance in revenues) and fixed costs of marketing capacity (variance in costs). As argued earlier, coping with such risks requires information, knowledge and experience.

10.6 Summary

Export marketing is about marketing across national borders. Dealing with customers in a foreign environment, with unfamiliar cultural, economic, legal, social and political systems, and with laws and regulations that may differ radically from those of the domestic market, poses serious challenges to businesses. The risks related to export marketing strategies can be mitigated by adopting systematic market selection strategies. This chapter presents a series of steps that marketing managers can adopt to improve their performance in foreign markets.

References

Albaum, G, Duerr, E., and Strandskov, J., (2005) *International Marketing and Export Management* -5th Edition (Pearson Education Ltd., England)

Cavusgil, S. Tamer and John R. Nevin (1981), "Internal determinants of export marketing behaviour: an empirical investigation" *Journal of Marketing Research* Vol. 28 No. 1 pp: 114-119

Cook, V.J., and Page, J.R., (1987) "Assessing Marketing Risk" *Journal of Business Research* Vol.15 No. 6 pp: 519 - 530

For Further Readings

Keegan, W.J. (1974) "Multinational Scanning: A Study of the Information Source Utilized by Headquarters Executives in Multinational Companies" *Administrative Science Quarterly* pp: 411-421

Kuada, John and Sørensen, Olav Jull (2000) *Internationalization of Companies from Developing Countries* (New York: International Business Press)

Mayer, C.S. (1978) "The Lessons of Multinational Marketing Research" *Business Horizon* pp: 7-13

CHAPTER ELEVEN

International Market Entry Modes and Global Strategies

11.1 Introduction

Selecting a mode of entry into a foreign market is among the most crucial strategic decisions a company can make. Weighing all factors and choosing the proper method can result in huge competitive advantages or it can cripple the organization. A market entry and development mode is defined as the institutional/organizational arrangement established to reach and cooperate with the foreign customers. Many entry modes require capital outlays and investments of some magnitude, e.g. the establishment of a sales subsidiary. Furthermore, it takes time to build solid and durable relations with foreign partners and, when established, the change of entry mode may have severe repercussions, (e.g moving from an importer to a wholly owned sales subsidiary may entail substantial investments). Establishing an entry mode is not just a simple marketing issue, but involves organizational and cross-cultural management issues as well, e.g. when cooperating with an importer or, more so, when establishing a strategic alliance.

This chapter provides an overview of the theoretical reasons underlying foreign market entry decisions that managers make. It starts with a description of the types of entry mode. It then discusses factors influencing entry mode selection decisions and how companies change their entry modes as their degrees of internationalization increases. It has been repeatedly argued that for different reasons many companies use multiple entry modes in their internationalization process. The final sections of the chapter discuss how companies respond to local particularities without losing their global focus and orientation.

11.2.   Market Entry Modes

Figure 11.1 provides an overview of the various types of market entry modes that have been discussed in international business literature. The three main categories are:

1. Export/Import, i.e. trading modes (Transaction modes)
2. Cooperation/Coalition modes (Transfer modes)
3. Foreign direct investment (FDI) modes (Transformation modes)

As companies grow bigger and extend their international outreach, they use a combination of entry modes, tailoring their choices to fit their own international business objectives and resources as well as the peculiarities of their host nations. The multiple modes they use might be tightly connected – i.e. the different modes tend to support each other in an overall foreign market penetration strategy (see Benito, Petersen, and Welch, 2009 for a discussion). Petersen *et al.* (2008) use the term ''mode configuration'' to refer to the diverse ways in which multiple modes might be configured or arranged, to develop a configuration matrix that includes different modes categorized by (value chain) activity level, governance form, and country. The three different entry modes are briefly presented in this section for a quick overview.

11.2.1 Exporting

Exporting allows companies to extend the life cycle of their current product line by selling them to foreign customers. This entry mode is often further categorized into direct or indirect export.

Direct Export: the organization uses an agent, distributor, or overseas subsidiary or acts via a government agency. Local agents or distributors are frequently used as intermediaries mainly because they have local knowledge, speak the language, understand the local business, and know who the customers are and how to reach them.

Indirect Export: products are exported through trading companies (common for commodities like cotton and cocoa), export management companies, piggybacking and counter-trade. The main advantage of indirect exporting is that the manufacturer/exporter does not need too much expertise and can count on trading companies and/or export management companies' knowledge.

In some situations, countries may enter into countertrade agreements on bilateral basis. There are two separate contracts involved in a countertrade, one for the delivery and payment for the goods supplied and the other for the purchase and payment for the goods imported. The seller, in fact, accepts products and services from the importing country in partial or total payment for his exports. This method is suited for situations where competition is low and currency exchange is difficult.

11.2.2 Contracting

A contract is a formal and binding agreement between two companies in which company "A" grants company "B" the right to produce and distribute goods normally produced by company "A"in the foreign market in return for some form of economic rents. Companies that have mature technology and greater levels of product standardization tend to favour contractual entry modes. The main forms of contractual agreements in international marketing are licensing and franchising.

Licensing allows another company (licensee) to use the technology or other knowledge resources that belong to the licensor in return for payment. Said differently, the company gives license to a foreign company that enables it to use, for example, manufacturing, processing, trademark, or name for selling purposes.

Franchising may be defined as a business arrangement which allows for the reputation, (goodwill) innovation, technical know-how and expertise of the innovator (franchisor) to be combined with the energy, industry and investment of another party (franchisee) to conduct the business of providing and selling of goods and services.

Franchisees are, in the majority of cases, people who have previously been employed by someone else and a franchise opportunity is seen as a more relaxed way of making the transition from working for an employer to being self employed. The risk factor of a proven business is also seen as a better option than breaking totally new ground. Most importantly though, franchises are invariably taken up by people who are prepared to invest in themselves, their personality and their skills - those fleeing the angst of office or corporate politics and looking for employment freedom and the rewards that hard work will bring. Compared to licensing, franchising agreements tends to be longer and the franchisor offers a broader package of rights and resources which usually includes: equipment, managerial systems, operation manual, initial trainings, site approval and all the support necessary for the franchisee to run its business in the same way it is done by the franchisor.

Strategic alliances constitute another form of contractual entry mode. The concept of strategic alliance is used in the management literature to cover a wide range of inter-firm collaborative arrangements (Yoshino and Rangan, 1995). It is characterized by collaboration, autonomy, accessibility of resources, and risk sharing between companies. The understanding is that collaborative arrangements are designed among companies whose resources are perceived by their managers to be complementary. Collaboration allows the partners to design coordinating mechanisms that enhance their joint ability to cope with market uncertainties. This in turn provides them with a foundation for establishing enduring relationships. Firms engaged in strategic alliances tend to maintain their operational and ownership autonomy, irrespective of the duration of their strategic relationship.

Alliance formation is presumed to proceed in two broad ways; either by planning or through an incrementally emerging process. The planning approach endorses the stage-like development of the alliances. The typical stages include 1) pre-partner identification stages during which a company acknowledges the need for a partner and specifies its partner choice criteria; 2) partner selection stage, where information is sought about potential partner companies and analysed in terms of the defined choice criteria and decision models; 3) courtship period when the selected partner is visited and the chemistry of collaboration process is tested and affirmed; 4) the negotiation process, where the strategic, organisational and legal framework for the collaboration is established; 5) the implementation process, where the rules of operation agreed upon are put into effect and adjusted to fit the practicalities of daily operation; 6) growth and intensive involvement stage, where performances are appraised and satisfactory results encourage further commitment and possible extension of domains of collaboration; 7) termination, representing a stage in which previous motives of collaboration no longer exist and new motives cannot be found to replace them (Kanter and Corn, 1994).

11.2.3 Foreign Direct Investments

A foreign direct investment (FDI) is usually defined as an investment made by a company based in one country, into a company based in another country. The following are the most common forms of FDIs:

1. Horizontal FDIs – where the company carries out the same activities in its foreign branches.
2. Vertical FDIs – where different stages of the value creating activities are added abroad to complement activities at home.
3. Conglomerates – where the company invests in unrelated businesses abroad.

In terms of investments, FDIs can either take the form of Greenfield investments or acquisitions of existing company (partially or fully).

Figure 11.1   Alternative Foreign Market Entry Modes

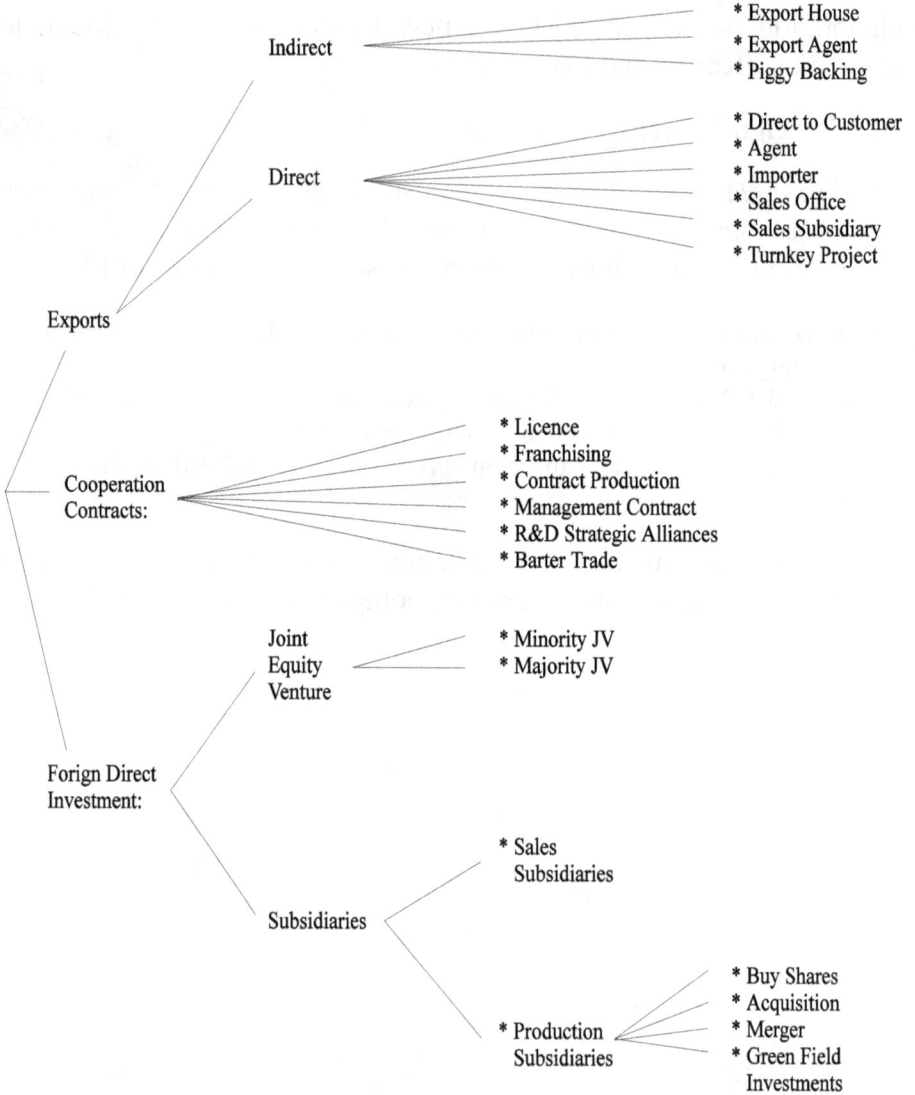

Indirect
* Export House
* Export Agent
* Piggy Backing

Direct
* Direct to Customer
* Agent
* Importer
* Sales Office
* Sales Subsidiary
* Turnkey Project

Exports

Cooperation Contracts:
* Licence
* Franchising
* Contract Production
* Management Contract
* R&D Strategic Alliances
* Barter Trade

Joint Equity Venture
* Minority JV
* Majority JV

Forign Direct Investment:

Subsidiaries
* Sales Subsidiaries

* Production Subsidiaries
* Buy Shares
* Acquisition
* Merger
* Green Field Investments

Source: Kuada and Sørensen (2000, page 56).

11.3 Ways of Choosing Market Entry and Development Modes

All entry modes involve some degree of investment. But the magnitude of the investments, their associated risks, and degrees of control vary with the choice of entry mode. The three interrelated key issues a company may have to deal with regard to its entry mode decisions are:

1. The choice of appropriate entry mode when entering a new market.
2. The change in entry mode when the companyincreases its degree of internationalization.
3. The management of a portfolio of market entry modes.

11.3.1 Choice of Market Entry Modes

Kuada and Sørensen (2000) offer the following five ways of deciding on which market entry mode to select:

1. Choice based on industry traditions
2. Unsolicited or reactive choices
3. Pre-determined choices
4. Contingency choice
5. Network-based choices

New entrants into an industry usually follow the traditions that exist in the industry in choosing their entry modes. Examples include the sales of agricultural products – especially food items – on the global market. Rules and regulations within the sector more or less define the distribution systems that new entrants may seek to use. This also creates problems of power and exlusion within the industry.

There are also situations in which companies initiate their exporting activities by filling unsolicited orders. By doing so, they implicitly or explicitly acknowledge the importer as their representative abroad. Reactive choice and the determined choices have their theoretical justification in the Internationalization Process (IP) theory propounded by Uppsala scholars (also popularly known as the stages theory of internationalization). It explains the internationalization process as incremental step-by-step approach. This implies that entry mode choices are path-dependent and change with the degree of internationalization of companies.

Empirically, the stages theory of internationalization is under heavy attack. Many claim that the uniqueness of each market at any point in time together with the exporter's resources and strategy, form the basis for the decision on market entry mode. In other words, the entry mode decision is contingent upon the specific circumstances. Thus, all options are open and the company analysts and planners will have to join forces to identify decision criteria and analytical tools in order to provide the decision maker with an assessment of the alternative entry modes. The criteria used for the choice of market entry and development mode will be company-specific. But the most commonly used criteria are:

- Financial risks involved by using a specific mode.
- Control over market activities.
- Cost efficiency.

Added to these, a company may also consider:

- Reversibility and/or exit costs.
- Feedback from the market, i.e. learning effects.

In practice, an entry mode is often chosen, not unsolicited and not following comprehensive planning, but based on the extension of existing networks of which the potential exporter is a member. That is, the new foreign partners are identified using the existing network, which serves as the springboard for new foreign ventures. It may be as simple as the company supplier having a contact abroad which can be approached, or an existing foreign customer in one country having contacts to some colleagues in one or several other countries.

The advantage of using the present network as a base for choosing new foreign partners is that the partners know each other well. The trust and mutual orientation that they have established from long-term cooperation, will enable firms within the network to work towards the attainment of each other's needs. Furthermore, using the network approach to choose entry modes reduces the costs of searching for new partners as well asthe risks of choosing the wrong partner.

As part of overall corporate planning, the strategic choice of entry modes aims to establish, maintain, and develop a viable fit between the organizational motives, objectives, and resources and the changing market opportunities (Young *et al*. 1989, p. 36).

Choosing entry modes according to the strategic choice model involves elements of, but goes beyond, the rational planning and cost minimization issues included in the contingency approach. For example, the strategic decision mode takes into account and anticipates reactions from rivals or it aims to be present in a market to assure access to knowledge and other resources. In other words, the strategic choice mode does not have the clarity and rigidity of the contingency approach. It is a pragmatic approach to decision making weighing subjectively a set of internal and external factors against each other. Rigid analytical tools from the contingency analytic tool-kit may, however, be used as an integrated part of the strategic choice mode.

Depending on the company's approach to corporate planning, entry modes may be chosen according to the strategic planning or the strategic management approach. The difference between the two is that the former has its strengths when complexity is relatively low and the environment stable while the strategic management approach is geared to situations characterized by complexity, uncertainty and diversity - a situation often facing the exporter.

11.3.3 Multiple Entry Mode Strategies

As companies become more internationalized and expand their geographical outreach and product portfolio it may be necessary for them to change from their original market entry modes in specific countries in order to more effectively and efficiently fulfill their customers' needs. Such changes are often very complicated, because they may involve the reshuffling of people. The more simple cases occur when a company realises that it has made a bad choice and thus needs to replace one agent or importer with another. The more complicated cases occur when a market grows and thus, the company would like to switch to a mode with a higher company commitment and control over the market activities, e.g. from an agent to a sales subsidiary.

Basically, the same five decision modes presented above can be used in changing a decision just as they have been used to make the initial decision. In case the company wants to shift, for example, from an agent to a sales subsidiary, because the market grows, it may, in order not to lose valuable market knowledge, offer the agent to become director of the subsidiary.

Apart from the problem of shifting from one mode to another, international companies often have to manage a portfolio of entry modes. This is confirmed in studies by Benito, Petersen and Welch (2009) showing that most companies adopt mode combinations at different points in the value chain in a foreign market, such as when a wholly-owned production subsidiary is supported by franchising at the marketing level. There is also evidence of mode combinations at the same point in the value chain, when sales in a foreign market are handled both by a sales subsidiary and an independent distributor: the sales subsidiary might be used to target large customers while the distributor handles disparate smaller customers; or the sales subsidiary handles sales in one geographical region of a country whereas other regions are the responsibility of one or more distributors. Benito, Petersen and Welch (2011) also found evidence of mode combinations that spread across activities in the same foreign market.

When a company uses different entry modes, the choice becomes more complicated. In principle, the optimal choice is made for each market. However, economies of scale, learning curves, synergies, etc. may make it more feasible to concentrate on certain types of market servicing modes.

11.4 Responding to Local Particularities

From an operational perspective, the extant literature is replete with the observations that global organizations strive to achieve behaviour al consistency across their affiliates. This explains why many scholars perceive organizations with global mindsets as those in which the underlying vision, values and management approaches found in a firm are widely shared and intensely held and orchestrated throughout the organization (Rhinesmith, 1996). Consistency in management practices in all affiliates is believed to speed up group action and create transnational cohesion based on an accepted corporate logic. However, it also means that the assumptions that govern the behaviour of employees are very rarely questioned. This, inevitably, blocks new learning and cuts down on the variety of perspectives brought to bear on management issues. It has, therefore, been suggested that global organizations must scout for novel ideas from near and wide and satisfy local needs in locally-appropriate ways in order to sustain their competitive advantages. Furthermore, empirical evidence suggests that management practices embedded in the home country's administrative heritage of MNCs are frequently rejected in host country subsidiaries when transferred there (Brock *et al.*, 2008). Thus, successful global organizations must learn to balance "global consistency with local responsiveness" (Begley and Boyd, 2003).

Perlmutter's (1969) ethnocentric, polycentric, regiocentric and geocentric management model has been frequently presented as an illustration of the challenges that companies face in deciding on the appropriate management practices to adopt globally. MNCs with ethnocentric orientation would want to transfer the rules of behaviour that are accepted and applied in the headquarters to employees irrespective of location. A polycentric company gives its subsidiaries wider degree of latitude to respond to changes in their environments. Its managers tend to think that host-country cultures and organizations have mindsets that are very different from theirs but equally valid in their unique contexts.

Neither ethnocentric nor polycentric orientations (in their pure forms) have proved to be successful management models in practice. Thus, the dominant view (echoed in several of the contributions above) is that mangers of multinational companies must combine high global integration with high local responsiveness in order to compete effectively in host country environments. This perspective is usually captured in the phrase "think global and act local" - the starting point being a global strategy focusing on standardization of rules of behaviour but allowing local adaptation, where appropriate.

The discussions in the previous chapters have inspired me to suggest an extension of the "think global and act local" guide in this chapter. I forward the view that organizations can address their integration-responsiveness challenges in four concurrent ways:

1. Think global and act global
2. Think global and act local
3. Think local and act global
4. Think local and act local

These four possibilities are illustrated in Figure 11.2

Figure 11.2: Thinking and Acting in Global and Local Contexts

<table>
<tr><td rowspan="2" colspan="2"></td><td colspan="2" align="center">THINK</td></tr>
<tr><td align="center">Global</td><td align="center">Local</td></tr>
<tr><td rowspan="4">ACT</td><td>Global</td><td>Supra- National Issues
E.g. Environmental sustainability</td><td>Innovation and Creativity
E.g. co-creation and sharing of knowledge</td></tr>
<tr><td>Local</td><td>Leadership and Human Resource Management Issues
E.g. expatriation</td><td>Marketing Issues
E.g. communication with customers & product adaptation</td></tr>
</table>

11.4.1 Think Global, Act Global

The first strategic option is to think and act global. MNCs may choose to think and act globally in relation to issues that are of global concern and require global strategies to address. A familiar example is global environmental protection issues that enjoin companies to formulate corporate social responsibility (CSR) strategies. The adoption of a CSR strategy that is applied in all affiliates of an organization serves to demonstrate corporate citizenship, with corporate image, goodwill and branding as outcomes (Irwin, 2003; Kuada and Hinson, 2012). The concept of shared value creation suggested by Porter and Kramer (2006), and Elkington's (1994) sustainable development perspective represent additional examples of the manner in which companies can both think and act global. Elkington argues that companies must assess their performance in terms of "the triple bottom line" (TBL) – i.e. profit, people and planet. In his view only a company that produces a TBL is taking account of the full cost involved in doing business. Thinking and acting in response to the challenges of the planet and people must be universal and consistency in doing so will improve an international company's overall profitability.

11.4.2 Think Global, Act Local

The second strategic option is to think global but act local. This is usually captured in the phrase "Unity without Uniformity". Some organizations seek to address the integration-responsiveness challenge by formulating superordinate vision or standardizing overall organizational values while allowing individual organizations to fit their strategies to specific local conditions. It requires the MNC to decide on which aspects of its values and practices it may universalize and which to particularize.

An example of a Danish company that has done this quite successfully may illustrate this option in practice. Since its establishment, the Danish toy company LEGO has pursued a consistent strategy in communicating its foundational principles and corporate identity to its affiliates and has therefore been successful in binding the company's business units into an integrated whole. Top management would want the LEGO name to be a universal concept associated with three notions: *ideas; exuberance*, and *values*. LEGO ideas are to be captured in concepts such as creativity, imagination, un-limitedness, and discovery. The notion of exuberance is also to be captured by concepts such as enthusiasm, spontaneity, and self-expression. The values come from concepts such as quality, caring, development, innovation and consistency. In other words, LEGO's brand identity has been based on abstract concepts although its original product – the brick toys - is tangible. The consistency between the brand image, the abstract concepts and the tangible product is seen in the design of the products - the flexibility that the bricks offer in construction stimulates children's imagination to combine the bricks in a wide variety of novel ways.

Since the early 1990s LEGO has ventured into three new and strategically important business areas: the LEGOLAND parks, lifestyle products and media products for children. In many cases these developments have entailed LEGO setting up a presence in countries outside Denmark. For example, in spring 2000, LEGO acquired a high-technology toy firm, Zowie Entertainment, in Mateo – about 30 kilometers from San Francisco. The American company specialized in innovative smart toys and with this acquisition LEGO made a big jump into the computer-driven toy sector. In order to integrate the new company into the LEGO family, the Danish headquarters encouraged Zowie Entertainment to develop and market its products in a way that is consistent with LEGO's underlying values. This was done through the formation of a number of task forces that aimed at providing employees from the headquarters and the new company with a mental space in which they could work together on joint projects. The headquarters' employees acted as carriers of the core values of the LEGO culture to the new environment. But together with the local employees they were encouraged to engage in new interpretations of these values within the local environment in order to achieve compatibility without sacrificing the underlying core principle of top quality, good service and creativity. Through these interactions employees from the headquarters and the acquired company were able to gradually challenge their respective comfort zones and at the same time avoid the destructive conflicts that personality clashes could produce.

11.4.3 Think Local, Act Global

This strategic option enjoins the MNC to develop structures and processes that encourage reverse learning - i.e. allow the companies to feed local experiences and lessons into the pool of internationally shared sources of knowledge. Previous studies of reverse knowledge flows have been focused on the types of knowledge that host country employees can provide expatriate who have been assigned to their organizations to train them and ensure that they abide by the corporate logic received from the headquarters. The understanding is that host country workers can help an expatriate gain cultural and contextual knowledge that can facilitate their interactions with the host society and improve their performance (Vance and Ensher, 2002). Later studies have shown that host country nationals also can effectively contribute to the pool of technical knowledge that helps develop new products for markets in different parts of the world. This emerging understanding draws on creativity theory. It has been argued that although creative breakthroughs may occur by chance, bringing ideas together from a variety of sources may speed up innovation processes in work organizations (Kuada, 2010). This requires that MNCs must be willing and able to receive and process knowledge gained from employees in host country organizations (Napier, 2006).

11.4.4 Think Local, Act Local

The "think local, act local" strategy implies understanding local needs and expectation and satisfying them fully at profit, drawing on available resources within the MNC. Companies have realized that no matter what mix of products, service and prices they offer in some markets, customers will have different perceptions of its value and remain not fully satisfied. This is a drawback on many local adaptations of global value propositions. In other words, there are situations in which companies still need to craft local solutions to local problems for them to effectively serve needs of local stakeholders and occupy a market space previously unexplored even by local firms. This requires giving local people the opportunity to analyze local needs using context-specific knowledge, enabling them to bring perspectives previously not considered in the operational history of the company to bear on the situations they identify by using corporate resources in novel ways. Hitherto, MNCs have shunned away from this approach, considering local adaptation as the most cost effective way of creating "local" value propositions. But as pockets of middle class consumers emerge and grow in the developing parts of the world, local-specific solutions are becoming profitable propositions that MNCs can hardly ignore. Further research is required to explore the usefulness of the "think local, act local" strategy to corporate performance.

11.5 Summary

Studies of companies' international market entry mode choices have been based on theories such as the stages theory of internationalization, the theory of International product/production life cycle (focusing on the changes in market entry/development modes over time) as well as the transaction cost theory and the eclectic FDI theory. The received understanding is that all entry modes decisions are guided by the types of industries that companies operate in, management strategic objectives, resources and degrees of risk and control they are willing to take. Choices are not static – they change with time and degree of internationalization. The exact composition of the portfolio of entry modes thus depends on the importance of the markets served andthe duration of time the company has had operations on the market as well as the characteristics of the host market environment (including governmental policies within each of the markets).

References

Begley, T.M. and Boyd, D.P. (2003) "The need for a corporate global mind-set", MIT *Sloan Management Review* Vol. 44 No.2 pp: 25 -32.

Benito, G.R.G., Petersen, B., and Welch, L.S. (2009) "Towards more realistic conceptualisations of foreign operation modes *Journal of International Business Studies* 40, 1455–1470

Brock, David M., Shenkar, Oded, Shoham, Amir and Siscovick, Ilene C. (2008) "National Culture and Expatriate Deployment" *Journal of International Business Studies*, Vol. 39, No. 8 pp. 1293-1309

Elkington, John (1994)"Towards the Sustainable Corporation: Win-Win-Win Business Strategies for Sustainable Development," *California Management Review* 36, No. 2 pp: 90 - 100.

Irwin, Ron (2003) "Corporate social investment and branding in the new South Africa" *The Journal of Brand Management* Volume 10, Number 4, 1 pp. 303-311

Kanter, R.M. & Corn, R.I. (1994) "Do cultural differences make a business difference? Contextual factors affecting cross-cultural relationship success". *Journal of Management Development*, Vol.13 No. 2 pp: 5-23.

Kuada, J. (2010). "Creativity and leadership in a cross-cultural context: the role of expatriates" In J. Kuada, & O. J. Sørensen (Eds), *Culture and creativity in organizations and societies* (pp: 9-23). (London, Adonis & Abbey Publishers Ltd.)

Kuada, J., & Hinson, R. E. (2012) "Corporate Social Responsibility (CSR) Practices of Foreign and Local Companies in Ghana" *Thunderbird International Business Review*, Vol. 54 No.4 pp: 521-536.

Napier, N.K., (2006) "Cross Cultural Learning and the Role of Reverse Knowledge Flows in Vietnam" *International Journal of Cross Cultural Management* Vol. 6 No.1 pp: 47 -64

Perlmutter, H.V. (1969) "The Tortuous Evolution of the Multinational Corporation", *Columbia Journal of World Business*, Vol. 4 No. 1 pp: 9-18

Petersen, B., Benito, G. R. G., Welch, L. S., &Asmussen, C. G. (2008) "Mode configuration diversity: A new perspective on foreign operation mode choice". In D. Griffith, S. T. Cavusgil, G. T. M. Hult & A. Y. Lewin (Eds), *Thought leadership in advancing international business research:* 57–78. (London: Palgrave).

Porter, M.E., and Kramer, M.R., (2006) "Strategy and Society: The Link between Competitive Advantage and Corporate Social Responsibility," *Harvard Business Review*, Vol. 84 No.12 pp: 78-92

Rhinesmith, S. H. (1996). *A manager's guide to globalization: Six skills for success in a changing world* (Second Ed.). (New York: McGraw-Hill).

Vance, C.M. and Ensher, E.A. (2002) "The Voice of the Host Country Workforce: A Key Source for Improving the Effectiveness of Expatriate Training and Performance" *International Journal of Intercultural Relations* Vol. 26 No. 4 pp: 447–61.

Young, Stephan, Hamill, J., Wheeler C., and Davies, J.R., (1989), *International Market Entry and Development: Strategies and Management*. (Englewood Cliffs: Prentice Hall).

For Further Readings

Kuada, John (2016) *Global Mindsets: Exploration and Perspectives* (London, Routledge)

CHAPTER TWELVE

Marketing in the Emerging Economies

12.1 Introduction

One of the fundamental developments in global marketing is the gradual shift of consumption centres from the developed economies to the big group of countries now labelled as emerging market economies (EMEs). Emerging markets have been at the top of growth projections in the global economy since 2010. In 2016 the euro area is projected to expand just 1.2 percent, U.K. by 2.5 percent and USA by 3 percent. In contrast, China and India's economies are expected to grow by 7 percent. Selected African countries are also among the high growth economies with Nigeria, Africa's largest economy, projected to expand by 5 percent, and Kenya growing by 6 percent. But recent trends indicate that aggregate annual GDP growth in the emerging market economies (EMEs) is expected to fall to around 4% in 2016 compared with the average of 7% in 2010. This decline is expected to continue for some time to come. The slowdown reflects the vulnerability of these economies to the general slowdown in the global economy. Many of them have depended on commodity exports such as oil for government spending that have cascaded through their economies and have fuelled domestic consumption. But as countries such as China have experienced slower growth and have transitioned into consumer-oriented economies, their demand for commodities have declined dramatically. Apart from the slow growth, there are some other serious marketing challenges partly due to uneven income distribution, poor public education, consistently high unemployment rates, a commodity driven economy, significant imbalance of market concentration and a large informal economy that hinders tax collection and keeps economic growth from reaching its full potential. Thus, the expectation that EMEs will continue to drive global consumption and economic growth has to be revised.

This chapter provides an overview of the growth trends in the EMEs and discusses their marketing implications. It first discusses the role of marketing in economic development process in general and then presents the international implications of these developments. The chapter then provides an overview of marketing opportunities and strategic options in some specific regions – Africa, Asia and Latin America. This is followed by some emerging marketing issues identified by practitioners and researchers with a focus on different segments of consumers in these regions.

12.2 Role of Marketing in Development Process

It is generally argued that marketing skills have played a major role in helping today's leading economies arrive at their current levels. In the same manner marketing can serve as the match that ignites the economic takeoff of developing countries (Arnold and Quelch, 1998). Building on this understanding, a group of researchers has examined the relationship between marketing and economic development and has provided policy guidelines on how marketing activities can be developed in the emerging market economies (Varadarajan, 1984). These researchers have seen marketing as performing both adaptive and formative roles in a country's development process, -i.e. marketing activities partly respond progressively to the development needs of an economy, and partly stimulate and reinforce the on-going change process in the economy (Kaynak and Hudanah, 1987; Kinsey, 1988). Another group of researchers has explored the opportunities and consequences of the transfer of Western marketing skills and technology to the developing countries. They see such Western marketing technology transfers as imperative for the development of the developing economies. The leading argument has been that the marketing systems in these economies must be modernized in order to serve the growing number of consumers in the countries (Drucker, 1958; Kaynak and Hudanah, 1987).

Previous research has revealed a general lack of appreciation of marketing's dynamic role by policy makers in these countries (see Kuada and Sørensen, 2000). Until the 1990s marketing intermediaries in most emerging market economies were viewed by the public officers as standing between consumers and the producers, and draining the economic system of vitality. As a result, market related policies tended to be rigidly regulatory and prohibitive, offering no inducement for the private sector to undertake investments in marketing facilities that could improve the coordination of activities within the national marketing systems (Abbott, 1987).

From a marketing perspective one of the special things about the EMEs that marketers must note is that consumers in most of the countries are 'leapfrogging' trends. For example, people are jumping straight from not having used technology at all to having smartphones and enjoying their usage in novel ways, unknown to consumers in the developed countries. For example, mobile pay has shown a widespread usage in countries such as Kenya before being adopted in by European consumers.

12.3 International Market Opportunities and Strategies

The contemporary literature on the internationalisation processes of firms discusses both downstream and upstream routes of internationalization (Kuada, 2016). Downstream internationalization addresses issues related to the involvement of companies in international market operations, whereas the upstream discussions relate to cross-border linkages initiated partly by local companies in order to strengthen their production processes and to leverage resources through joint tasks, input deliveries, as well as upgrading their technological and managerial capacities. We have earlier noted that exports constitute the first step in the downstream internationalization process. At the macroeconomic level, exporting contributes to foreign exchange reserves of nations, provide employment and foment forward and backward linkages within an economy. At the micro level, export marketing provides firms with new market opportunities and thereby raises their capacity utilization, improves their financial positions and overall competitive positions. The small size of local demand of most developing countries further justifies their reliance on export-led growth strategies.

Three conditions allow some developing country companies to engage in downstream internationalisation without any prior or significant upstream activities. The first is their inclusion in the international value chains of lead companies. Research work on the electronics industry and contract manufacturing in Asian countries (Sturgeon, 2002), the apparel industries in Asia (Gereffi, 1994) and Africa (Gibons, 2001) as well as the horticultural industry in Africa (Dolan and Humphrey, 2000) provide empirical evidence of these forms of export marketing activities of emerging market companies. Second, producers of ethnic products that have differential advantages due to unique design can target niche market in Europe and North America. Examples include *kente* from Ghana (Kuada and Sørensen, 2000) and utilitarian handicrafts from different developing countries. Third, several developing countries have embarked on export-led growth strategies that provide special locational incentives to local firms as well as locally-based foreign firms in export zones to produce for export.

But due to a multiple set of reasons, developing country companies' export marketing processes are severely constrained and can be extremely slow at best. The export marketing literature contains a long list of factors – both external and internal - that inhibit developing country companies' export activities. The external factors include high relative cost of financing exports (Bilkey, 1978; Czinkota and Ricks, 1983), dealing with bureaucracy within public agencies (Rabino, 1980; Cavusgil, 1984) export documentation (Rabino, 1980; Czinkota and Ricks, 1983), lack of market information (Katsikeas and Morgan, 1994), logistical constraints and high cost of transportation (Rabino, 1980). The internal constraints include difficulties in meeting importers' quality standards (Rabino, 1980) export packaging (Czinkota and Ricks, 1983), lack of competent staff (Kothari and Kaynak, 1984) and inability to self-finance exports (Bilkey, 1978). Foreign distributors may hesitate to buy from developing country companies due to constraints listed above. In addition to these, the literature has identified supply side constraints such as limited capacity of suppliers to fulfil pre-shipment value-adding requirements of distributors abroad as severely reducing the attractiveness of these firms as exporters to Europe and North America.

A company may initiate its internationalization process by first importing inputs from a target country. The inputs may be necessary to raise the added value of the export products. Furthermore, the import arrangements will provide the firm with some international exposure prior to its subsequent export marketing activities. Information about market opportunities abroad may be generated through contacts that it makes by importing inputs. Having a position within an international business network as a buyer, management finds it relatively easier to explore opportunities in these markets for its products. Thus, market selection flows naturally from these initial contacts.

Entering and succeeding in EMEs can be tough. Poor infrastructure, bureaucracy and protectionist policies constrain market penetration and success may depend on a big dosage of flexibility, creativity and entrepreneurial drive. Brazilians have a complex culture, consumer mindset and media landscape, but if marketers take a close look at the forces shaping Brazilian society in tandem with political, economic and social shifts, they can effectively lay the groundwork for a strong performance in this growing market.

Studies have shown that the best-performing companies in these economies adopt the same market-driven strategies as in the high-growth economies - i.e. they compare their marketing against their best-performing peers and adopt marketing mix strategies that differentiate their value propositions from their competitors. Sales personnel are encouraged to spend sufficient time with customers, become more focused on execution and customer satisfaction. They are also expected to adopt systematic methods in identifying capability gaps they need to close (and to close them in the right sequence) in order not to overstrain their resources. The marketing goals of the successful companies have also been noted as being "slow growth with high margins". This requires them to focus their marketing efforts a lot more on the needs and preferences of the high-end consumers. There is also a need to ensure that the companies' operating models are just right.   An operating model needs to be specific and measurable, including elements such as clear annual performance-improvement goals; scheduled and formal reviews throughout the year by segment, key account, and other categories.

12.4 Some Regional Opportunities and Challenges

12.4.1 Africa

Africa's economic growth trends in recent years have shown that the continent has been infused with new consumer optimism. The continent's growth reached 4.8% in 2013 (from 4.2% in 2012) and is expected to accelerate to 5 % in 2016 (World Bank, 2015). Out of 54 countries, 24 of them more than doubled their per capita income over 1990–2010 (African Development Bank Report, 2014). In 2015, seven of the 10 fastest-growing economies in the world are in Africa. Demographic trends also favour market growth in Africa. By 2050 the current 1 billion people is expected to double and 1billion of them will be under 18. Consumer spending on the continent is expected to increase to nearly $1 trillion by 2020 (Hattingh *et al.*, 2012). It is also estimated that by 2022, more Africans will move out of poverty to become middle-income consumers, granting that economic policies can be crafted to provide the young people with the education and skills they need to contribute effectively to economic growth. Thus, the general assessment is that, while short-term risks remain, Africa has strong long-term growth prospects, propelled both by external trends in the global economy and internal changes in the continent's societies and economies. It has also been suggested that since marketing is concerned with the satisfaction of needs and wants and the optimum allocation of resources, if used effectively, it can raise productivity and enhance economic growth.

However, strategic marketing processes and priorities remain poorly understood in Africa and, the impact of politically powerful coalitions on market development policies remains strong (Chelariu *et al.*, 2002; Winston and Dadzie, 2002). The potential role of marketing in Africa's economic growth and poverty alleviation therefore remains largely unexplored.

12.4.2 Asia

Asia's rising influence in the global economy is attributed mainly to the size of its economy and consumers. In 1990, Asia's share in world GDP in real US$ purchasing power parity (PPP) was 23.2 percent. By 2014, this went up to 38.8 percent, much larger than the shares of the United States and the European Union. Thus, during the past two decades Asia (particularly the Eastern part) has become one of the main growth drivers of the world economy, accounting for about two-fifths of global economic growth. The region is expected to grow at 6.5% in 2016 with countries such as China expected to grow at about 7%. The projections also show that if current growth trends in key regional economies continue Asia's share in world GDP is likely to go up to nearly 45 percent by 2025.

Economic growth has been fuelled more by infrastructural investments than consumption. While consumption's share of GDP in Europe and North America is about 70, it is in the neighbourhood of 30 in such countries as China. It means that stimulation of consumption in high growth Asian countries will be an important contributor to global economic growth. The expectations are that the segment of society that is under 25 years demonstrate a higher propensity to consume and may be more readily stimulated to increase their consumption. By the mid-2020s, this segment of the society is expected to account for 30 to 40 percent of consumption spending. International marketing practitioners are realizing that performance depends on the ability of companies to understand the local tastes and preferences and to design products and services to satisfy them. For all but a few categories, volume (rather than a high profit margin) is a winning strategy.

Another important development that marketers are mindful about in these parts of the world is the increasing urbanization and its marketing implications. Studies in different parts of the world have shown that cities are by far the dominant nodes of mass consumption. These consumers have been dubbed "citysumers". They are described as being more open-minded than other segments of their populations. They are also more socially connected, more spontaneous, and more willing to try new products irrespective of their countries of origin.

Following studies by McKinsey there is a correlation between the sizes of cities in Asia and the spending habits of people living in them. For example, studies have shown that people who lived in Beijing, Shanghai, and other first-tier cities tended to buy similar products. Marketers will therefore need to fine tune their strategies to meet their needs. Urban consumers have been described as sophisticated who frequent well-known stores that have quality customer services, when compared with their rural counterparts in the same country. They have also shown themselves to be active users of mobile technology allowing marketers to target them with communication strategies via mobile devices. This means that for brands, delivering city-specific products, services and communications that truly capture a city's character is an excellent way to build recognition and trust. Some practitioners suggest that urban consumers are especially receptive to brands that use daring and edgy marketing campaigns and strategies.

12.4.3 Latin America

During the beginning of the 21st century, Latin America became a marketer's dream region, partly because of its size, and partly due to its economic growth. It was estimated that by 2020, the region will represent 10% of the global population and 9% of global GDP, with 640 million customers. But this promising development trajectory appeared derailed by recent trends. Since 2013, the economies have been experiencing low growth averages, of about 2% to 2.5% of GDP. In 2016 there was no positive turnaround at sight. The IMF said in its 2015 regional forecast that the major economies in the region, including Brazil were experiencing the most serious economic downturn in more than two decades, with output projected to fall by 1 percent in 2015. The deceleration is linked to decreasing commodity prices, a slower Chinese economy, and shrinking investments.

From a marketing perspective, the region is considered rather heterogeneous. Trade rules, customs and geography vary across the region, and languages spoken include everything from French, English and Dutch in the Caribbean to dozens of other languages in Central and South America. Thus, what works in one Latin American country has been found not to work well in another. But one pattern common across

Latin America is a sharp gap between rich and poor. About 15% of the people can be classified as belonging to the upper or upper-middle classes, and another 20 to 40 percent fall in the middle class. That leaves about 50 to 65 percent of the population in the lower classes. Many companies adopt a "high margin, low volume" strategy, targeting the 15% upper-class consumer segment with luxury items. A few companies target the bottom of the pyramid, using a "low margin, high volume" strategy. They do so by re-packaging popular premium brands of products such as toothpaste or laundry detergent in smaller containers. This makes quality products accessible to people in the lower consumer segments.

12.5 Some Emerging Issues and Research Opportunities

12.5.1 Country-of-origin and Marketing

Since the beginning of the 1970s an increasing number of products from developing countries have been appearing on the global marketplace. These products come from three main categories of companies: 1) subsidiaries of multinational corporations (MNCs) which establish offshore production facilities in developing countries (Dunning, 1988), 2) joint venture firms between developed and developing country firms (Beamish, 1988), and 3) exports from developing country firms themselves (Kuada and Sorensen, 2000). The increasing popularity of trade liberalization policies and export-led growth strategies of the developing countries implies that developing country firms will compete with established international firms for the attention of global consumers. Some of these companies export hybrid products; i.e. acquiring the design and parts from developed country companies and producing them in the emerging market economies. For this reason, Chao (1993), and Tse and Lee (1993) have argued for the decomposition of product images into relevant country-of-origin (COO) dimensions. It has been proposed that the various country information to which consumers is exposed may interactively affect their product evaluations and perceptions (Sauer, Young and Unnava, 1991). That is, if the country enjoys a positive image, all the COO dimensions will reinforce consumer perception of the product (Chao,

213

1998). In the same vein, if the COO dimensions are different (i.e. the product design, assembly and parts come from three separate countries) the different source images may compensate for each other. For example, poorer product quality perception due to association of a product with a negative assembly COO location stereotype may be enhanced by a more positive parts COO location stereotype. Similarly, a poorer product quality perception due to association of the product with a negative parts COO location stereotype may be compensated by a more positive assembly COO location stereotype.

Few empirical investigations of hybrid product-country linkages have hitherto been conducted in the emerging market economies and their marketing strategy implications addressed.

12.5.2 Ethnocentrism and Marketing

Ethnocentrism is a sociological concept, which describes the superior sentiments that a specific group of people hold about the culture and ways of behaviour of their own group (the in-group) in comparison to those who are not members of the group (Ardono *et al.*, 1950). This concept has been introduced into the marketing literature to describe consumers' attitude towards products from their own country in comparison with similar products from other countries. Shimp and Sharma (1987) define consumer ethnocentrism in the United States of America as "beliefs held by American consumers about the appropriateness or morality of purchasing foreign products". They then used a 17-item scale, to measure the extent to which American consumers feel that buying foreign products is unpatriotic or immoral because of its adverse impact on jobs and the economy. In other words, ethnocentric consumers are inclined to view purchasing of imported products as wrong as it hurts the domestic economy and is not congruent with their in-group feelings of patriotism and belongingness to their societies. Other scholars have suggested that ethnocentrism is positively associated with other domination ideologies such as nationalism, xenophobia, and social dominance orientation (Altintas and Tokol, 2007). Their argument is that ideology feeds nationalism and thereby ethnocentrism. Thus, Han (1989) suggests that ethnocentrism may have its root causes in nationalism. Consumer

214

behaviour scholars have, therefore, used ethnocentrism to describe consumers' belief that locally produced products are superior to imported products (Shimp and Sharma, 1987; Herche, 1992; Saffu and Walker, 2006; Saffu and Scott, 2009). In a similar manner, Shankarmahesh (2006) has argued that socio-psychological constructs, such as animosity, materialism, dogmatism, as well as economic and political parochialism reflect consumer ethnocentrism.

These discussions will imply that ethnocentric tendencies may impact the manner in which domestic and foreign companies design their marketing strategies when operating in the emerging markets. For example, if consumers in the given country are highly ethnocentric, it would be advantageous for domestic marketing managers to undertake a promotional campaign that stresses a nationalistic theme (Saffu and Walker, 2006). But if ethnocentric tendencies are weak, it may be important to emphasize product attributes such as quality in marketing communication strategies rather than relying on consumers' nationalistic-based loyalties. These considerations are important for both local and foreign companies.

12.5.3 Marketing and Bottom of the Pyramid (BOP)

Recent studies elsewhere have linked marketing to poverty alleviation through the popularization of the *bottom of the pyramid (BOP)* framework presented in the works of such scholars as Prahalad and Hammond (2002), Prahalad (2005), Hart and London (2005), as well as Kotler and Lee (2009). Ideas contained in these studies tend to suggest that some of the successful marketing strategies that impact poverty may appear to be in conflict with the dominant logic that has guided marketing practices in the developed parts of the world. In the developed countries, firms adopt marketing strategies that are aimed at targeting selected market segments and gaining market shares. In other words, firms seek to serve existing demands for their goods and services and they see consumers' purchasing power as an indicator of market size and attractiveness of potential markets. That is, the presence of unfulfilled needs among groups of people does not constitute demand in the conventional marketing sense. The bottom of the pyramid perspective challenges this notion of demand and its related strategies and calls on firms to engage in market expansion for overall growth purposes (i.e. undertake demand creation) rather than adopting selective marketing strategies. This will help speed up overall market growth in a given country.

There are distinct differences between a market-based approach to poverty reduction and more traditional approaches. Traditional approaches often focus on the very poor, proceeding from the assumption that they are unable to help themselves and thus need charity or public assistance. A market-based approach starts from the recognition that being poor does not eliminate commerce and market processes: virtually all poor households trade cash or labour to meet much of their basic needs. A market-based approach thus focuses on people as consumers and producers and on solutions that can make markets more efficient, competitive, and inclusive—so that the BOP can benefit from them.

Traditional approaches tend to address unmet needs for health care, clean water, or other basic necessities, by setting targets for meeting those needs through direct public investments, subsidies, or other handouts. The goals may be worthy, but the results have not been strikingly successful. A market-based approach recognizes that it is not just the very poor who have unmet needs - and asks about willingness to pay across market segments. It looks for solutions in the form of new products and new business models that can provide goods and services at affordable prices.

12.6 Exploring New Potentials of Marketing in Emerging Economies

It has also been noted above that a customer-oriented marketing management is based on market analysis which provides firms with a better understanding of customer needs, expectations, behaviour as well as their current and lifetime value to companies. But what happens when customers do not know what they really need or what types of products and services can raise their quality of life and therefore cannot communicate their demands to businesses? Recent thoughts in the marketing literature have suggested that it is better for firms to adopt "market-driving" strategies in such situations. That is, they must be bold enough to be a step ahead of their potential customers.

As noted above, conventional marketing logic tends to consider many EME consumers as being too poor to be viable customers. Prahalad (2005) has a different perspective. He estimates that the poor people of the world have buying power equal to $8 billion per day. This makes the poor a multi trillion-dollar annual market on a global scale. For example, considering the fact that the African population is growing rapidly and is expected to be two billion within the next three decades, businesses can hardly afford to ignore even the poor segments of the population. Kotler and Lee (2009) convey the same perception when they argue that the poor have the right to want what the rich want and, as a group, they constitute incipient demand waiting to be tapped. One of the immediate marketing challenges is to make existing products and services accessible to these segments of the population and thereby draw them into the monetized segments of the economies.

Following Prahalad (2005), this may require the adoption of product modification strategies, including innovative packaging techniques that sell some consumer goods in smaller units and at affordable prices without lowering their qualities. It may also require marketers to see consumers not as individuals but as groups and to develop marketing packages for households, villages and communities. In this light, Hart and London (2005) advise foreign companies that intend to take advantage of the business opportunities that poverty provides to become "indigenous" or "native" to the places in which they operate. Doing so will require deeper insights into the dreams and behaviours of the local people.

Furthermore, it is important to bear in mind that poverty is more than just a lack of income. It also connotes lack of respect, self-worth, dignity, inclusion, choice, and security (Hart and London, 2005; Kotler and Lee 2009). Poverty makes people to resign to their living conditions (Letelier, *et al.*, 2003) and holds their creativity in check. Thus, poverty sets negative spiral in motion. This means any effort made to alleviate poverty is itself growth-propelling since it unleashes hitherto untapped psychological and physical human resources within a community and thereby helps transform a negative spiral into a positive one. Poverty alleviation is therefore not a philanthropic project but a viable business proposition. Thus, marketing strategies that expand consumption also create mechanisms for enhanced business performance.

Leaning on this perspective, it appears to me that businesses in EMEs must adopt both market-driving and market-oriented strategies. It is necessary for businesses to tap into global knowledge base and apply them to develop products and services that will not only serve the immediate consumption needs of EME consumers, but also enhance their productivity as well. Academic research is required to provide firms and institutions with useful knowledge that can guide their policy and strategy formulations that impact on growth and poverty alleviation. By bringing some of the above perspectives on board, researchers will not be studying marketing and economic development as isolated fields of research but will focus on the links between them.

12.7 Summary

The global economy has witnessed a substantial shift in consumption centres from the developed economies to the emerging market economies. This has introduced new dynamics into the international marketing process with companies having to adjust their strategies to new and hitherto unknown realities. The growing populations in these parts of the world are sources of new market opportunities. But they also pose new challenges due to their individual peculiarities. Nearly all of them are characterized by uneven income distribution, poor public education, consistently high unemployment rates, commodity driven economies, and large informal economies. Entering and succeeding in these markets therefore call for new strategic thinking in the areas of new product development and marketing. The chapter provides suggestions on how companies may address these challenges and enjoy the potential benefits that the markets provide.

References

Abbott, John C., (1987) *Agricultural Marketing Enterprises for the Developing World* (Cambridge: Cambridge University Press)

Adorno, T. W., Frenkel-Brunswik, E., Levinson, D.J. and Sanford, R. N. (1950), *The Authoritarian Personality,* Oxford, England: Harpers.

African Development Bank (2014) *The bank's human capital strategy for Africa (2014 2018)* OSHD Department, May 2014

Altintas, M.H. and Tokol, T. (2007), "Cultural openness and consumer ethnocentrism: an empirical analysis of Turkish consumers", *Marketing Intelligence & Planning,* Vol. 25, No. 4, pp. 308-325

Arnold, D. J. and Quelch, J. A. (1998) "New strategies in emerging markets" *Sloan Management Review* Vol. 40 No.1 pp: 7-20.

Beamish, Paul W. (1988), *Multinational Joint Ventures in developing Countries.* Routledge, London.

Bilkey, Warren J., (1978) "An attempted integration of the literature on the export behaviour of firms" *Journal of International Business Studies* Vol. 9 No. 1 33-46

Cavusgil, S. Tamer (1984) "Organizational characteristics associated with export activity" *Journal of Management Studies* 21, 1 pp: 3-22

Chao, Paul (1993), "Partitioning Country-of-Origin Effects: Consumer evaluation of a Hybrid Product," *Journal of International Business Studies*, 24(2), 291-306.

Chao, Paul (1998), "Impact of Country-of-Origin Dimensions on Product Quality and Design Quality Perceptions," *Journal of Business Research*, 42(May), 1-6.

Chelariu, C., Ouattarra, A., and Dadzie, K. (2002), "Market Orientation in Ivory Coast: Measurement Validity and Organizational Antecedents in a sub-Saharan African Economy," *Journal of Business and Industrial Marketing*, Vol.17 No.6, pp. 456-470.

Czinkota, Michael R. and D. A. Ricks (1983) "The use of a multi-measurement approach in the determination of company export priorities" *Journal of the Academy of Marketing Sciences* Vol. 11 No. 3 pp. 283 - 91

Dolan, Catherine and Humphrey, John and Harris-Pascal, Carla (1999) "Horticulture Commodity Chains: The Impact of the UK Market on the African Fresh Vegetable Industry" IDS Working Paper 96 University of Sussex, UK

Drucker, Peter F., (1958) *Technology, Management & Society* (New York and Evanstone, IL: Harper & Row)

Dunning, John H. (1988), "The Eclectic Paradigm of International Production: A Restatement and Some Possible Extensions" *Journal of International Business Studies*, Vol. 19 No.1 pp: 1-31.

Gereffi, G. (1994) 'The organization of buyer-driven global commodity chains: how U.S. retailers shape overseas production networks', in G. Gereffi and M. Korzeniewicz (eds) *Commodity Chains and Global Capitalism*, Westport: Praeger, pp. 95-122.

Gibbon, P. (2001) 'Upgrading primary products: a global value chain approach', *World Development* 29 (2): 345-63.

Hart, Stuart L. & London, Ted (2005) *Developing Native Capability: What Multinational Corporations Can Learn from the Base of the Pyramid* (Stanford: Stanford Social Innovation Review)

Han, C.M. (1989), "Country image: halo or summary construct?", *Journal of Marketing Research,* Vol. 26, No. 2, pp. 222-229.

Hattingh, D., Russo, B., Sun-Basorun, A., and Van Wamelen, A (2012) *The Rise of the African Consumer* (London, McKinsey Company)

Herche, J. (1992), "A Note on the Predictive Validity ofthe CETSCALE", *Journal of the Academy of Marketing Science,* Vol. 20, No. 3, pp. 261-264.

Katsikeas, Constantine S. and Robert E. Morgan (1994) "Differences in Perceptions of Exporting Problems Based on Firm Size and Export Market Experience" *European Journal of Marketing* Vol, 28 No. 5 pp: 17-35

Kaynak, E., and V. Kothari (1984) "Export behaviour of small manufactures: a comparative study of American and Canadian firms" *European Management Journal* Vol. 2 summer pp: 41-47

Kaynak, E. and Hudanah, Ben Issa (1987) "Operationalizing the relationship between marketing and economic development: some insights from less developed countries" *European Journal of Marketing* Vol. 21 No. 1 pp 48-65

Keillor, B.D. and Hult, G.T.M. (1999), "A five country study of national identity: Implications for international business research and practice", *International Marketing Review,* Vol. 16, No. 1, pp. 65-82.

Kinsey, Joanna (1988) *Marketing in Developing Countries* (London, Macmillan Education Ltd.)

Kotler, Philip and Lee, Nancy R., (2009) *Up and Out of Poverty* (Upper Saddle River, New Jersey Pearson Education, Inc)

Kuada, J. and Sørensen, Olav Jull (2000) *Internationalization of Companies From Developing Countries* (New York; London : International Business Press)

Kuada, John (2016) "Internationalisation of Firms in Developing Countries: An Integrated Conceptual Framework" In Kuada, John *Perspectives on International Business – Theories and Practice* (London, Adonis & Abbey) pp: 71 - 98

Letelier, M. F., Flores, F., and Spinosa, C., (2003) "Developing Productive Customers in Emerging Markets." *California Management Review* Vol.45 No. 4 pp77-103

Prahalad, C. K., & Hammond, A. (2002) "Serving the world's poor, profitably." *Harvard Business Review* Vol.80 No.9 pp: 48-57.

Prahalad, C. K. (2005) *The Fortune at the Bottom of the Pyramid: Eradicating Poverty Through Profits* (Upper Saddle River, NJ: Prentice Hall)

Rabino, S. (1980) "An examination of barriers to exporting encountered by small manufacturing companies" *Management International Review* Vol. 1 pp: 67-73

Saffu, K. and Walker, J. (2006), "An Assessment of the CETSCALE in a Developing Country", *Journal of African Business,* Vol. 7, No. 1, pp. 167-181.

Saffu, K. and Scott, D. (2009), "Developing country perceptions of high- and low-involvement products manufactured in other countries", *International Journal of Emerging Markets,* Vol. 4, No. 2, pp. 185-199

Sauer, Paul L., M.A. Young and H.R. Unnava (1991), "An Experimental Investigation of the Process Behind the Country-Of-

Origin Effect," *Journal of International Consumer Marketing* 3(2), 29-57

Shankarmahesh, Mahesh N., (2006) "Consumer ethnocentrism: an integrative review of its antecedents and consequences", International Marketing Review, Vol. 23 Iss: 2, pp.146-176

Shimp, T. and Sharma, S. (1987), "Consumer Ethnocentrism: Construction and Validation of the CETSCALE", *Journal of Marketing Research,* Vol. 24, No. 3, pp. 280-289.

Sturgeon, T. (2002) "Modular production networks: a new American model of industrial organization", *Industrial and Corporate Change* 11 (3): 451--496.

Tse, David K. and Lee, Wei-na (1993), "Removing Negative Country Images: Effects of Decomposition, Branding, and Product Experience" *Journal of International Marketing,* 1(4), 25-48.

Varadarjan, Rajan P. (1984) Marketing in developing countries: the new frontier" *Long Range Planning* Vol. 17 No. 6 pp 118-126

Winston, E., and Dadzie, K. (2002), "Market Orientation of Nigerian and Kenyan Firms; The Role of Top Managers," *Journal of Business and Industrial Marketing*, Vol.17, No.6, pp. 471-480.

World Bank (2015) *Global Economic Prospects*, (Washington, DC: World Bank)

For Further Readings

Vernon-Wortzel, H., Wortzel, L.H., and Deng, S (1988) "Do neophyte exporters understand importers?"*Columbia Journal of World Business* Vol. 23 No. 4 pp. 49-56

Wang, J. (2005), "Consumer nationalism and corporate reputation management in the global era", *Corporate Communications: An International Journal,* Vol. 10, No. 3, pp. 223-229.

Wortzel, Lawrence H. and H. Vernon Wortzel (1981), "Export Marketing Strategies for NIC and LDC-Based Firms" *Columbia Journal of World Business*, 16 (Spring), 51-60.

CHAPTER THIRTEEN

Societal and Ethical Considerations in Marketing Decisions

13.1 Introduction

In addition to its economic implications, marketing exerts a significant impact on the values of the society. There has, therefore, been a growing interest in issues of social responsibility and ethics in business since the 1990s. Different studies have suggested that individuals' world outlook, willpower, courage and personal integrity combine with corporate values and identity to influence the degree to which ethical and social considerations are factored into business decisions. But there are still pronounced disagreements among scholars about the potential usefulness of different social and ethical policies and strategies for enhancing companies' performance. The accepted understanding is that variables such as differences in the operational contexts of firms, sizes, types of organisation, and ownership exert different degrees of influence on companies' social practices.

The debate has hitherto pitched the *stockholder theorists* against the *stakeholder theorists* – i.e. those who see social and ethical concerns as distracting businesses from their cardinal goals on the one hand, and those who see them as providing superior legitimacy to businesses within their ambient societies. The advocates of socially responsible marketing argue that marketing strategies may create false wants, i.e. encourage people to buy more than they actually need, inject constant desire for material possession and lead to excessive spending. Too much obsession with material goods in the long run may cause damage to the society as a whole. Thus, socially responsible marketing draws attention to "social costs". This chapter provides an overview of the debate and highlights its implications for marketing decisions. It starts by introducing readers to the concept of corporate social responsibility (CSR) and the theoretical arguments underlying it. It then discusses the link between CSR and marketing decisions.

13.2 The Concept of Corporate Social Responsibility

The academic debate on corporate social responsibility (CSR) started with a denial that businesses need to concern themselves with social responsibilities at all. This perspective was put forward very forcefully in the writings of Friedman (1962) who argued that the business of business should always remain business and social concerns are antithetical to sound business practice and serve to dilute business focus on wealth creation. In his view, there is only one social responsibility for business – i.e. to use its resources and engage in activities designed to increase its profits so long as it stays within the rules of the game, meaning to compete openly without deception and fraud. Thus, although companies can have legal responsibilities, they do not have moral responsibilities since they are not human beings.

Other scholars have vehemently argued against Friedman's position and endorse what is referred to in the literature as the stakeholder perspective on business. The protagonists of this perspective see business and society as interwoven rather than distinct entities (Wood, 1991). In their view, businesses are active partners in a world of increasing scarcity and dwindling resources. That is, being principal creators of economic value in modern societies, businesses have obligations to contribute not only to the wealth of stockholders but to the welfare of other citizens of societies in which they are located (Jamali and Mirshak, 2007). Thus, Bowen (1953:6) defined CSR as the obligation "to pursue those policies, to make those decisions, or to follow those lines of action which are desirable in terms of the objectives and values of our society". Carroll (1979) suggests that different types of social obligations can be distinguished: (a) economic obligations (be productive and economically viable), (b) legal and ethical obligations (follow the law and acknowledged values and norms), and (c) philanthropic obligations (proactively give back to society). These perspectives are predicated on the understanding that CSR practices are motivated by self-interest: they enable businesses to gain legitimacy among their constituents.

Maignan and Ferrell (2004) propose the notion of stakeholder orientation as a useful concept to grasp the degree to which a company understands and addresses stakeholder demands. In their view, a stakeholder orientation is composed of three sets of behaviours: (a) the organization-wide generation of intelligence pertaining to the nature of stakeholder communities, norms, and issues, along with the evaluation of the firm's impacts on these issues; (b) the dissemination of this intelligence throughout the organization; and (c) the organization-wide responsiveness to the concerns of stakeholders. In presenting the stakeholder perspective, Freeman (1984) argued that whilst organisations were undoubtedly established with the help of equity provided by shareholders, the conduct and success of their operations are also dependent upon the participation and actions of various other stakeholders, like customers and suppliers, employees and workers, lenders, governments, regulatory authorities, communities and societies and the larger ecological environment. This means that organisational managements are obliged to satisfy shareholder expectations through the enhancement of organisational market share, profitability, dividend payouts and wealth. At the same time, it is their professional obligation to ensure that the other stakeholders (who directly or indirectly contribute to their success) also benefit from the wealth that they create. It has also been argued that it is not unusual for the operations of companies to produce adverse environmental consequences in the form of air, water and land pollution, deforestation, waste generation and emission of greenhouse gases (Freeman *et al.*, 2004). Negative workplace practices and unethical marketing practices (e.g. Nestle's persuasion of mothers in developing countries to replace breast feeding with the use of the company's powdered milk products) have also been cited as inimical to corporate legitimacy.

Since Freeman's earlier works on CSR, other concepts have emerged in the literature to reinforce the arguments that he advanced. Some scholars see CSR as reflecting corporate citizenship, corporate philanthropy, corporate giving, and corporate community involvement – emphasising the social role on its own merit. Others see these practices as corporate social investments (Babarinde, 2009) with corporate image, goodwill, and branding as outcomes (Irwin, 2003). Value-led branding is therefore catching on as a deliberate corporate strategy that should provide increased returns on investment and is measured along the same lines as other forms of economic investments.

Following Kotler and Levy (1969) some of the benefits of being socially responsible include (a) enhanced company and brand image (b) easier to attract and retain employees (c) increased market share (d) lower operating costs and (e) easier to attract investors. A socially – responsible firm will care about customers, employees, suppliers, the local community, society, and the environment. Porter and Kramer (2006) argue that "successful corporations need a healthy society" and in turn "a healthy society needs successful companies," and thus there is an interdependence between the two.

13.2.1 The Legal Demands in CSR

Following Idemudia (2008) three perspectives have emerged in the CSR debate at the beginning of the 21st century: (1) the voluntary initiative perspective, (2) the accountability perspective, and (3) the enabling environment perspective. Regarding the first, scholars such as Mathew (2004) argue that CSR initiatives are most effective when they are voluntary rather than obligatory. While government regulations interfere with corporate freedom and undermine efficiency, voluntary self-regulation in organisations is intrinsically motivating to organisational members. The accountability perspective presents contrasting arguments. Its proponents argue that the logic of capitalism does not support CSR initiatives. As such, businesses should not finance CSR activities and sacrifice their profits unless compelled by laws and regulations to do so. Legally binding local and international regulations are therefore necessary to ensure that businesses take social responsibilities seriously and deliberately design strategies to promote such behaviour. The third perspective suggests that although the voluntary initiatives and legally binding obligations are necessary, they do not provide sufficient conditions for the fulfilment of national and international expectations of CSR (Garvin *et al.*, 2009). There is therefore the need for governmental institutions, non-governmental organisations and civil societies to join hands to create incentives and congenial environments that stimulate CSR initiatives. Without joint planning and actions, key stakeholders may end up undermining each others' efforts (Gulbrandsen and Moe, 2007).

13.2.2 The Ethical Arguments in CSR

The economic drivers of CSR are reflected in the corporate social investment literature referred to above. The legal triggers imply expectations that firms play by the legal "rules of the game." From this perspective, society expects business to fulfil its economic mission within the framework of legal requirements. The ethical responsibilities of firms define expectations that are not stipulated in laws but are considered in a given society as being part of the morals, ethos or accepted rules of behaviour for firms and organisations. These responsibilities are predicated on the view that managers are guided in their decisions by high moral codes of conduct - doing only what is right, just, and fair. In specific terms businesses are expected to engage in behaviours such as respecting people, avoiding social harm, and preventing social injury (Lantos, 2001). Thus, the World Business Council for Sustainable Development (WBCSD, 2000) defines CSR as achieving commercial success in ways that honour ethical values and respect people, communities, and the natural environment. Similarly, Steiner and Steiner (2000) argue that social responsibility is the duty a corporation has to create wealth by using means that avoid harm, protect, or enhance societal assets. Finally, the discretionary perspective sees some CSR responsibilities of firms as volitional or philanthropic in nature and rooted in altruistic principles. That is, some companies may accept some social responsibilities beyond the expectations of their stakeholders or what members of the ambient societies consider as being ethically appropriate.

13.3 Corporate Social Responsibility and Marketing

Socially responsible marketing emerged as a response to questionable marketing practices that have adverse effects on society. The major economic criticisms that the conventional private marketing system receives from are as follows: First, mainstream marketing strategies generally lead to high prices. Due to the size of the chain of intermediaries in marketing, the distribution of commodities to consumers costs a lot. As a result, individuals pay higher premiums for the goods and services that they receive. Second, contemporary marketing relies heavily on aggressive advertising and promotion. In order to offset the costs, companies charge higher prices through excessive markups. Third, product differentiation is one of the most commonly used marketing tools. But this does not only create an artificial psychological value attached to higher-priced brands but also raises environmental concerns about packaging. As such, socially responsible marketing rejects all deceptive marketing practices in pricing, promotion and packaging, even if they may seem technically legal.

This enthusiasm for corporate social responsibility has been echoed in the marketing literature. Marketing scholars' concern about CSR in the 1970s has been limited to the social duties attached to the marketing function and not on the overall social role of companies (Maignan and Ferrell, 2004). The current view is that shared standards of acceptable behaviour should guide all marketing decisions. In this light, marketing now raises some of the most widely and hotly disputed ethical issues regarding business. Whether it is advertising, retailing, pricing, marketing research, or promotion (to name just a few marketing areas), marketing has been charged with engaging in practices that involve dishonesty, manipulation, invasion of privacy, creating unsafe products, as well as the exploitation of children and vulnerable consumers.

13.4 Tripple Bottom Line and Business Performance

The development of the Tripple Bottom Line represented the first attempt by CSR advocates to scientifically articulate the dimensions of CSR from the perspective of specific organisational responsibilities, actions and reporting processes (Elkington, 2004, p 21). As noted in chapter eleven, the Tripple Bottom Line (TBL) concept stated that organisational focus in business must take account of profitability and at the same time go beyond it to deal with the requirements of the planet and people (Elkington, 2004, p 21).

Thus, the concept articulated the 3Ps (profit, people, and planet) responsibilities of business companies and stated that organisations should achieve objectives in these three areas. It means the performance of businesses must not only be measured in terms of profits to stockholders, but must be concurrently assessed in terms of the impact of their operations on people within and outside the companies as well as the planet in general. In other words, companies must earn profits, because such profits are essential for further growth and even survival. But earned profits should be reasonable, just, and not earned at the cost of various other stakeholders, especially the community and the environment. Furthermore, companies operate through the actions of employees and provide their products and services to other people. As such, it is the responsibility of businesses to safeguard the interests of all persons that they relate directly to – i.e. within and outside the companies.

The accepted view in the practitioner literature is that the TBL model provides a sound basis on which management can plan and implement its CSR strategies and communicate the outcomes in a convincing narrative to stakeholders at large. This form of performance measurement provides stronger basis of legitimacy to its marketing practices. It can also go a long way in promoting both customer and employee engagement. Put differently, incorporating TBL in a business model acts as a mechanism to reach out to the public in new ways; ways that get people talking, sharing and ultimately consuming more. Projecting the image of ethical practices such as sustainable sourcing, fair treatment of employees and being charitable, can focus the public's spotlight onto these praiseworthy policies and consequently onto companies from which they come.

13.5 Greenwashing and Corporate Social Responsibility

One of the biggest issues that a company which engages in CSR practices for marketing purposes should be concerned with is greenwashing and how stakeholders will be affected by such practices. The concept of greenwashing covers situations in which companies use strong marketing tools to deceive the public into thinking that they are engaging in genuine CSR strategies without actually doing so. For example, if a company can certify their product as "green," they gain a certain degree of competitive advantage over their competitors and many customers will be more willing to buy their product than one that has not been certified as "green," because they perceive the value of the product to be higher than others. But if such a certification is shown to be false it can have nearly irrepairable consequences for corporate image.

Thus, the development of successful CSR marketing strategies may start with internal education and engagement. Employees must be convinced that top management is committed to its CSR rhetorics and that initiatives taken are real and genuine – i.e. not sheer greenwashing. It may also be helpful to focus on a handful of key opinion leaders in the social space that can carry the company's message and help elevate the company's profile within the stakeholder community. Doing this effectively involves moving away from a top-down strategy determined by the board to a richer process of bottom-up co-creation with stakeholders. It means using focus groups and other marketing research techniques to understand the deeper psychological needs that corporate responsibility can answer for stakeholders, such as the self-esteem and pride that a consumer can draw from affiliating with a socially responsible company. With such knowledge companies can elicit and gauge the demands of their target audiences.

13.6 Summary

There is an unsettled debate between protagonists and antagonists of the stockholder perspective in business. The protagonists of the stockholder perspective argue that businesses' primary function in societies is to provide a return on investment to owners and shareholders, create jobs and fair pay for workers, and discover new resources. Anything more than that imposes unfair burden on businesses. Those opposing this perspective argue that companies have a responsibility to maintain an equitable and working balance among the claims of various stakeholders (stockholders, employees, customers and the public at large). The current emerging practitioner view is that CSR is the continuing commitment by business to behave ethically and contribute to economic development while improving the quality of life of the workforce and their families as well as of the local community and society at large. In its broadest categories, CSR typically includes issues related to: business ethics, community investment, environment, governances, human rights, market place and workplace.

While the companies and critics each present compelling arguments for or against CSR, it may be that corporate social responsibility is just a negotiated balance between companies and the communities in which they operate. The challenge for management is to balance the needs of all stakeholders with their companies' need to make a profit and reward their shareholders adequately.

References

Babarinde, Olufemi A (2009) "Bridging the economic divide in the Republic of South Africa: A corporate social responsibility perspective" *Thunderbird International Business Review* Vol. 51, Iss. 4; p. 355- 368

Carroll, A. B.: (1979). "A Three-Dimensional Conceptual Model of Corporate Performance" *The Academy of Management Review* Vol. 4 No.4 pp. 497–505

Elkington, John (1994)"Towards the Sustainable Corporation: Win-Win-Win Business Strategies for Sustainable Development," *California Management Review* 36, No. 2 pp: 90 - 100.

Freeman, R. E., Wicks, A. C. and Parmar, B. (2004) "Stakeholder Theory and 'The Corporate Objective Revisited'", *Organization Science,* Vol. 15 No. 3, pp. 364-369

Friedman, M. (1962) *Capitalism and Freedom,* University of Chicago Press, Chicago, IL,

Garvin, T., McGee, T.K., Smoyer-Tomic, K.E., Aubynn, E. A., (2009) "Community-ecompany relations in gold mining in Ghana" *Journal of Environmental Management* Vol. 90 pp: 571-586

Gulbrandsen, Lars H., and Moe, Arild (2007) "BP in Azerbaijan: a test case of the potential and limits of the CSR agenda?" *Third World Quarterly* Vol. 28 Issue 4 pp: 813 - 830

Idemudia, Uwafiokun (2008). "Conceptualising the CSR and Development Debate- Bridging Existing Analytical Gaps" *The Journal of Corporate Citizenship,* Vol. 29 Spring pp: 91- 110

Irwin, Ron (2003). "Corporate social investment and branding in the new South Africa" *Journal of Brand Management* Vol. 10, Issue 4, pp 303-311

Kotler, P. and Levy, S. J. (1969) "Broadening the Concept of Marketing", *Journal of Marketing,* Vol. 33, Jan., pp. 10-15

Jamali, Dima and Mirshak, Ramez (2007) "Corporate Social Responsibility (CSR): Theory and Practice in a Developing Country Context" *Journal of Business Ethics* 72 pp: 243- 262

Lantos, G.P (2001). "The boundaries of strategic corporate social responsibility" *Journal of Consumer Marketing* Vol. 18 No. 7, pp. 595-630

Maignan, I., and Ferrell, O.C., (2004) "Corporate social responsibility and marketing: An integrative framework" *Journal of the Academy of Management Science* Volume 32, No. 1 pp 3-19

Mathew, P. (2004). "The Need for a Balanced Debate" *The Spark: Engineers against Poverty Newsletter* Available at www.engineersagai nstpoverty.org/docs. Assessed on June 4, 2009

Porter, M.E., and Kramer, M.R., (2006) "Strategy and Society: The Link between Competitive Advantage and Corporate Social Responsibility," *Harvard Business Review*, Vol. 84 No.12 pp: 78-92

Steiner G., and Steiner J., (2000) *Business, Government and Society: A managerial perspective:* (Boston, McGraw-Hill)

Wood, D. (1991). "Corporate Social Performance Revisited" *The Academy of Management Review* Vol. 16 No. 4 pp: 691-717

For Further Readings

Basu, K., & Palazzo, G., (2008), "Corporate social responsibility: A process model of sense making", *Academy of Management Review*, Vol. 33: pp. 122-136.

Bowie, N., (1991), "New directions in corporate social responsibility", *Business Horizons*, Vol. 34, Iss (4): pp. 56-65.

Brown, D., Dillard, J., & Marshall, R. S., (2006), *"Triple Bottom Line: A business metaphor for a social construct"*, Portland State University, School of Business Administration, Available at:www.recercat.net/bits tream/2072/2223/1/UABDT06-2.pdf (accessed April 13, 2014).

David, P., Kline, S., & Dai, Y., (2005), "Corporate social responsibility practice, corporate identity, and purchase intention: A dual-process model", *Journal of Public Relations Research*, Vol. 17: pp. 291-313.

Index

www.ingramcontent.com/pod-product-compliance
Lightning Source LLC
Chambersburg PA
CBHW061158220326
41599CB00025B/4526